To Nolan &
his family

Merry Christmas
from Ann

MAKING THINGS

MAKING

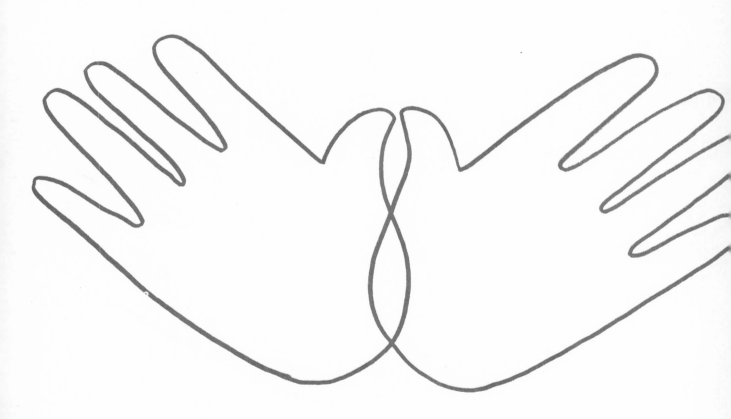

The Hand Book of Creative Discovery

THINGS

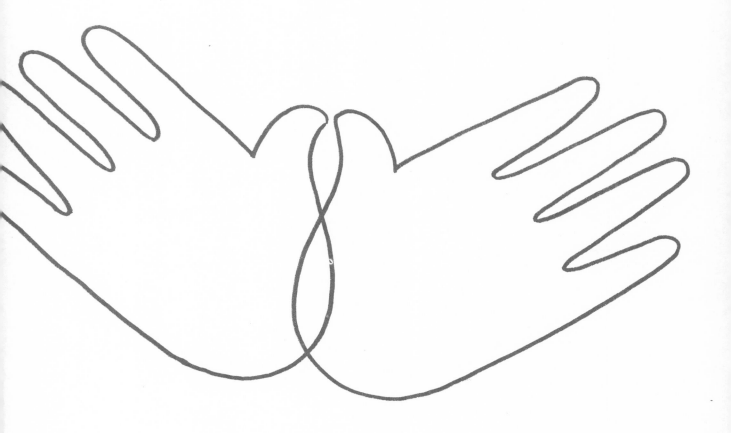

by **Ann Wiseman**

Little, Brown and Company
Boston Toronto

Acknowledgments for permission to reprint previously copyrighted material appear on next page

Acknowledgments

The author is grateful for permission to base a few ideas included in this book on material from the publications or demonstrations of:

The Boston Children's Museum and Resource Center, especially Bernard Zubrowski for his giant bubbles.

Education Development Center, inc., for the emergency hammer, the conduit pipe xylophone, the coat hanger bow drill (developed by Nat Burwash), the thumb piano adaptations and bubble launching.

Margaret galloway for measurements and directions for the shepherd's pipe, taken from her book, Making and playing Bamboo Pipes (which also includes alto and tenor measurements). Published by Dryad press, Leicester, England, 1958; new edition 1973.

Taplinger Publishing Co., Inc., New York, for the paper faces, from the book Paper Faces by Michael grater. copyright © 1967 by michael grater.

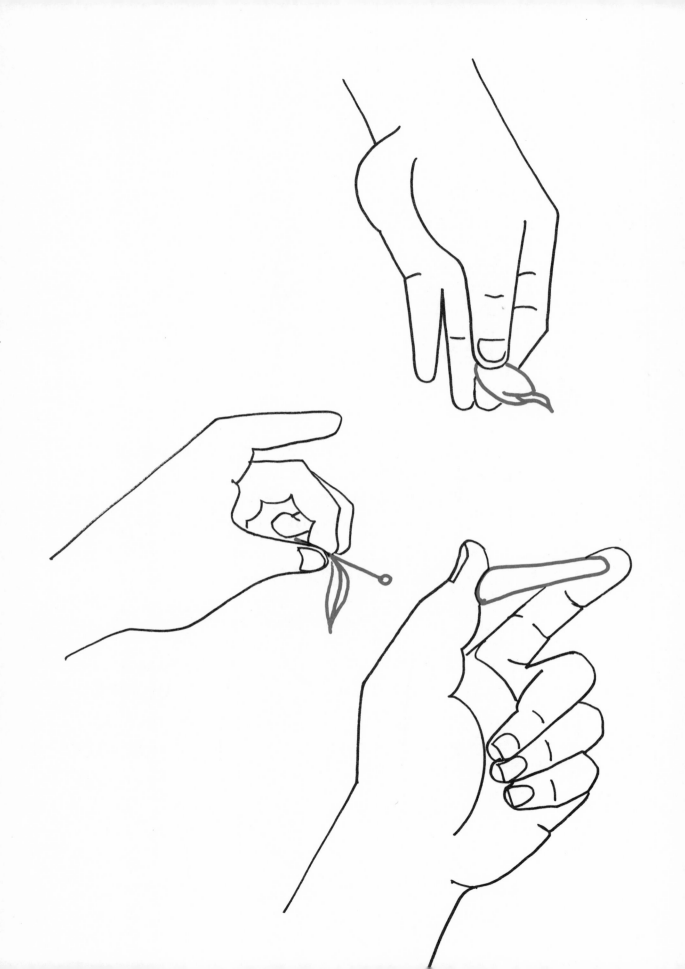

this book is
dedicated to
The Opposable
Thumb

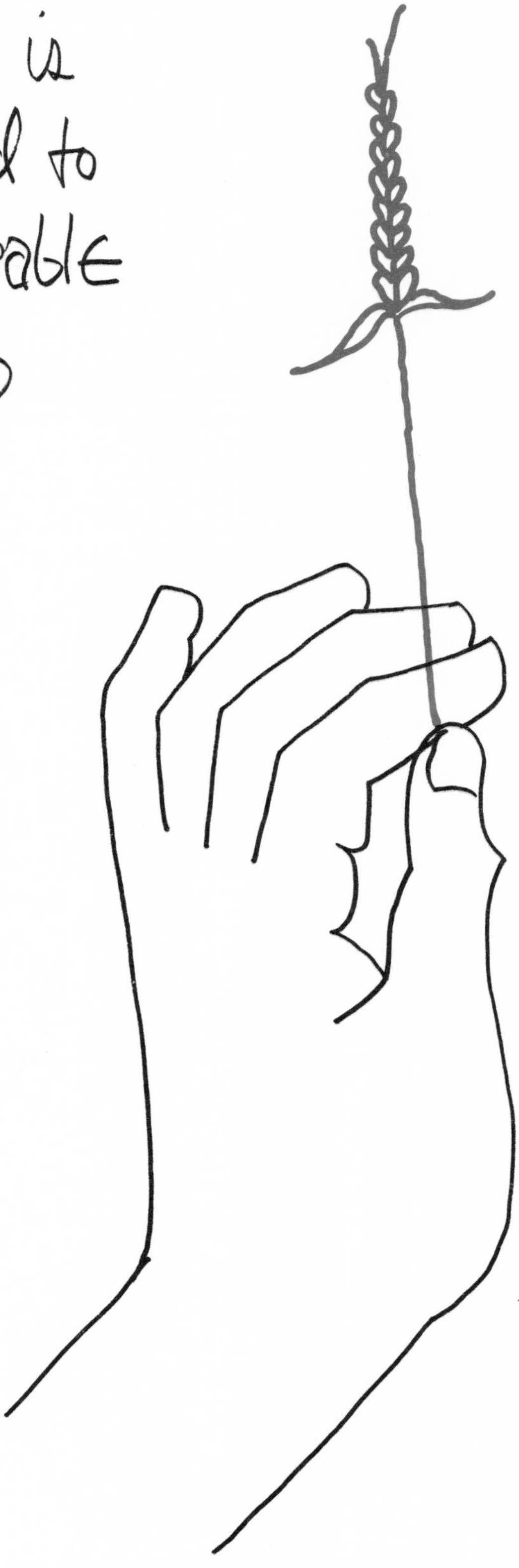

that
unique
bonus
available
to man.

2 Introduction
4 Dear Beginners
7 Save
9 Learning by doing
10 Originals
12 Questions & Solutions
14 Paper making
16 Paper Lace Hangers
18 Paper ornaments
20 Paper cutting
21 Paper Cone Sculpture
22 3-D Lift up Village & City
24 Fold & Cut
26 Paper curls & mobiles
27 Tissue Fish
28 Paper gliders
29 Paper spinners
30 Paper Faces
32 Finger Puppets
34 Paper bag Puppets
36 Corrugated cut-away
38 Finger Printing
40 Printing Vegetables
42 Owl business
44 Roller Printing
45 Printing Potatoes
46 Block Printing
48 Fish Printing
50 Finger Painting
51 Chocolate Pudding Prints
52 Painting
53 Color chart
54 Window Shade Maps & Murals
56 Crayons
57 Rubbings
58 Slotted Animals
59 Kiko's Seagull
60 Bed Friends
61 Pillow Cozies
62 Appliqué & Stitchery

64 Portable Houses
65 Box Houses
66 Piet's Horse Bench
67 Box Horse
68 Skate Skooter
69 Go-cars
70 Stilts
72 Grandfather's Willow Whistle
73 Pocket Wonders
74 Emergency Hammer
75 The Little Hack saw blade
76 Alaskan Bow Drill
77 Coat Hanger Bow Drill
78 Grass Hats & mats
80 Leaf Skeletons
81 Weed Keeper
82 Animated motion
83 Movies
84 Kites · Kites · Kites
86 Cardboard racing Turtles
88 Twisting
89 Rope Winding
90 Over & under weaving
91 Heddle
92 Plastic Drinking straw Belt Loom
93 Popsicle Stick Heddle loom
94 Box & Stick Inkle Loom
95 Tying Heddle Loops
96 Weaving in Math
97 Weaving the Binomial Theorem
98 Weed weaving
100 Macramé · Sailors Lace
101 Easy macramé 4 string belt
102 Macramé necklace sampler
103 Macramé Love Pouch
104 Bo'sun's Keel Loom
106 Rya Tufting
107 Tufted Shaggy vest
108 Body Covering
109 Body Logic clothes

110 Quick Clothes
112 Tie-dye
114 Quick Batik
116 Foot Gloves
118 Stocking Masks
120 Box Costumes
121 Box Sculpture
122 Odd Sock Puppets
123 Odd Glove Finger Puppets
124 Unusual Bubbles
126 Avocado Pear Tree
128 Casting Plaster
129 Sand Casting
130 Plaster Scrimshaw
131 Plaster Carving Blocks
132 Conduit Pipe Xylophone
133 Sweet Sounds
134 Thumb Piano · Kaffir
135 Shepherds Pipe
136 Tin Can Lanterns
137 Tin Lid Ornaments
138 Climbing Pull Toy
139 Flapping Owl
140 Hammered Wire Jewelry
141 Neck Hooks
142 Love Beads
143 Pasta & Paper Clips
144 Balance & Gravity
146 Salt Pendulum
148 Candle Dipping
149 Candle Casting
150 Stained Glass Cookies
152 Baker's Clay
153 Bread Sculpture
154 Peaceable Bread
156 More Art & Craft books
158 Books on ways of learning
160 Never End.............
162 Index

MAKING
THINGS

The wonder and understanding of simple beginnings-
the fabric of living and life-skills is the art
of human ecology and the balance of sanity.

We have been so distracted and astounded by our
technical achievements that in our excitement
we foster specialization and reap distortion,
rendering ourselves less than human.

Specialization may be the path to eventual
extinction and in our impatience to exceed
human limits we devise force-feeding methods
in the name of education to prepare our
children for our passions; but they, lacking
our particular motivation, find it quite
indigestible and unpalatable. This packet of
knowledge is often substituted for healthy normal
growth.

For centuries most of our schools have served
as centers that warped as well as shaped
the human spirit according to the needs of
the times and the system in vogue.
Children have been stuffed with unrelated
information and facts, out of which only a
few tid-bits fall into useful service.

The phenomenon of learning belongs to the
child, not to the teacher. We do not teach
a child to walk — one of many skill potentials
innate in all beginners. At best we stimulate
discovery, desire and curiosity, encourage
and whet the appetite, provide space, and
anticipate readiness to exercise the inevitable.

2

Learning by experience is profound knowledge, more deeply recorded in the memory than theory or speculation. Children left to their own devices will show you how they learn. The most direct, immediate and satisfying path to knowledge is visual and manual experience linked with the urgency of interest. A good teacher will find it or create it.

Information-gathering, based on personal motivation, is in fact the best tool the teacher has to open paths of learning. But those essentials may be shy or frail in children who are pressured and bent for reasons they don't comprehend.

In all cases it is a great help to have as many resources at hand as possible, as the hands lead the way to learning and logic. The hands absorb and transmit undescribable messages and information to the brain in the most thorough way available to us. Yet we often limit the hands of the school child to the stultifying dimensions of a pencil, a ruler and pages of a book.

This collection of discoveries and resources is a winnowing of simple and important concepts that have shaped the cultures of man. Children should find it full of revelations and adventures in wonderful logic, experiences both concrete and abstract. They are explained in pictures, so children just starting out and grown-ups who have missed out can quickly grasp the ideas.

But it is especially meant for parents and teachers who hold the success of children in their tone of voice and generosity of understanding.

3

Dear Beginners and Other people
remember that you know
more than you think you know.
And what you know now will
be stronger and longer in your
memory bank than anything
else you will ever learn.

When you have done
everything in this book, you
will have taught your hands
lots of useful things for pleasure
necessity, leisure and survival.

These are concepts and skills that should set your imagination free and welcome your own variations.
  Ask questions
  Experiment in safety
  Learn by doing
  Believe in yourself
And you will be better equipped to enjoy the natural wonders which are here if we have eyes to see and hands to know.

"play is very serious business"
        Erik Erikson

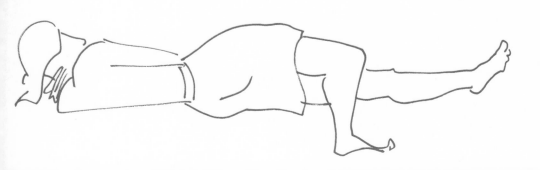

Credits and thanks

How does one thank all the people over the years whose imagination, research or necessity gave birth to the wondrous ideas collected in this book?
I can only mention my sources and hope the original or unknown discoverers will feel thanked by the thousands of children who will share these revelations.

Idea collecting started, for me, in the 3's 4's and 5's at Caroline Pratt's _City and Country School_ in New York City where we learned by doing. We visited factories to find out how things worked. School was a workshop based on necessity and logic, with time for experimentation and imagination and exercises in creativity, adaptation and improvisation.
Later in Elizabeth Irwins _Little Red School House_ on Bleecker Street we lived history and practiced the skills of the early peoples.

It was my privilege to participate in the _King-Coit children's theatre_ where Dorothy Coit and Edith King transformed French romances, Persian Legends, Blake's poems and little children into living works of art. And work under Victor D'Amico at The People's Art Center and Holiday Circus at _The Museum of Modern Art_ in N.Y.C. And not to forget Huey McCort's window display _carpentry shop at Lord & Taylor's_ N.Y.C. where a solution was always available even to impossible ideas.

My thanks to anonymous teachers and passing colleagues, but especially my grandfather Louis Sayre who built sailing ships in his cellar and read us Swiss Family Robinson. And more recently, numerous innovative developers, inventors, designers, master teachers from _Education Development Center_ and _The Workshop for Learning Things_: Nat Burwash, Phylis Morrison, George Cope, John Merrill and from The _Boston Children's Museum_ where innovation is collected and recycled by people like director Mike Spock's staff which has included: Allan Conrad, Becky Corwin, Bernie Zubrowski, Steve Caney, Maurie Sagoff, Dave Twitchell, Signe Hanson, Jan Spalvins, Fred Kresse, Cynthia Cole, Elaine Gurion, Clara Wainwright and many others. Thanks to instigators of ideas like Louise Tate dir. of _The Mass. Council of the Arts & Humanities_, Dr. Alice Baumgarner consultant, and _The N.H. Commission on the Arts_, who sponsored my explore & experience program in mixed media for elementary school teachers.
And special thanks to my boys _Piet and Kiko_ who have participated and improved many ideas. And to The _Michael Karolyi Memorial Foundation_ in Vence France for gentle refuge and time to draw this book.
AW. Vence France 1972

SAVE

Egg cartons   for seed growing, lanterns, sorters
plastic containers   for storage, weaving frames
babyfood jars   for storage & sorters & bead keepers & paint
plastic straws   for weaving looms, construction, gliders etc.
Styrofoam meat trays   for paper-making, printing & mobiles
shoe boxes   for sand-casting, dioramas, looms, silk screen
old lampshade wire   for tubular macramé, bubble frames, mobiles
wood scraps   for looms, block-printing, carving & building
shirt cardboards   for weaving looms, slotted animals, turtles
buttons & beads   for macramé, stringing & games
nuts & berries   for stringing and games & planting
empty thread spools   for ink stampers & pulling toys
inner tube tires   for cutting relief patterns for roller printing
magazines   for collage, mosaics, & paper beads
sticks & dowels   for Inkle looms, kites, paint stirrers
tongue depressors   for hole & slot heddle looms
tooth picks   for construction and building
old window shades   for "wall-windows" & roll-up murals, maps
fabric scraps   for rug hooking & braiding, rag tapestries
tin cans & lids   for ornaments & lanterns
colored telephone wire for jewelry, weaving & sculpture
big gallon cans   for "foot-raisers," templates & lanterns
milk cartons   for bathtub boats, bird feeders, planters
refrigerator cartons   for walk-in houses & puppet theatres
nylon stockings   for puppets, see-through masks & weaving
odd socks & gloves   for hand and finger puppets
gallon mayonnaise jars for moss gardens & batik dye savers
clothes pins   for dolls and box animal legs
wire clothes hangers   for bubble frames & stocking mask frames
soup bones   for scrimshaw scratching & napkin rings
chicken bones   for cut bone beads
   etc. etc. etc. etc. etc. etc. etc. etc.

I hear

and I forget

I SEE

and I remember

I DO

and I understand

LEARNING BY DOING

Learning by doing breeds creative thinking, self-expression, and the confidence to experiment, control, and perfect skills.

The thrill and wonder of discovery can be the starting point for self-propelled information gathering, leading to all the other disciplines and preparing a receptive and logical foundation for learning.

By encouraging self-discovery, originality, and individualism we avoid the competitive atmosphere and expect each participant to proceed at his own pace.

A workshop of activities such as these can be a contagious place for idea seeding and spreading; a laboratory for the development of natural curiosity and experimentation.

We hope to excite new ways of seeing, feeling, and being, in order to preserve the innate creative potential in every one of us.

If children of the stay-at-your-desk era instead of being punished for their energy, had been given interesting outlets – the art of spit balls would never have become the major creative pastime of the public school system.

Original · Original · Original

If you think that we are each Original combinations of genes that have never existed before you must pause with wonder as a new child strives to become himself.

But in our haste to get things done, be efficient, save time, keep the schedule and avoid harm

unknown to be discovered · unknown · To be discovered

Original · Original · Original · Original

We rush children through childhood.

For we are a very busy culture with little time for quiet thought or contemplation.

It takes immense patience to allow children to learn at their own pace and through their own mistakes.

Perhaps it is only vanity for us to think we can better past cultures by jumping to maturity without having exercised growth.

unknown · To be discovered · unknown · To be discovered

Questions

"What'll I do?" —

    usually said by children - freely translated means ... what CAN I do that won't be <u>duty</u>, make a <u>mess</u>, <u>waste</u> materials, get in <u>your way</u> or require me to <u>wait</u> (which is real punishment for a young child full of excited curiosity and instant appetites).

"Will you show me how?"

    means .. please stop, go slowly and make it clear so I too can <u>own</u> this skill, and do it well, all by my self!

"Is this right?"

    means, is it as good as yours, <u>or</u> do I have <u>permission to Experiment</u> and will you give me approval even if it isn't Just like yours.

"Thank you for Showing me" & "I can do it"

    means: you have given me the gift of myself - I needed help finding <u>me</u>.

Solutions

Needed: an enlarged expansive attitude towards space. Tolerance for mishap or arrangements to accommodate it. EVERY WORK PRODUCES WASTE — incorporate the idea, anticipate the inevitable.

Stop : simplify, explain the logic — it helps understanding and heightens interest. It's easy if _child independence_ is truly your goal.

Right by whose standards? what is right? The right that makes things work, please, or improve. Give permission to experiment — that is RIGHT.

Provide ways to develop independence and self-reliance, pride of accomplishment, and self-expression — a good self-image.

PAPER MAKING

5 MINUTE RECYCLE RECIPE : makes new grey sheets
(a little detergent added to the water helps bleach newsprint ink :)

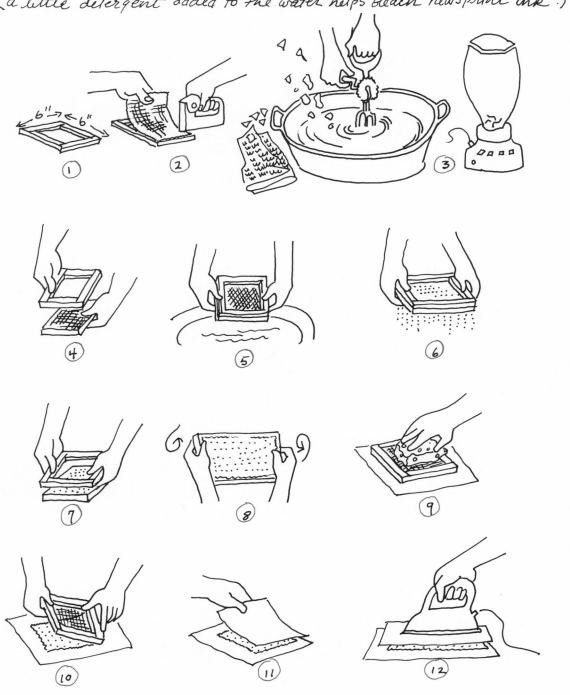

draw a picture or write a poem to someone you love.

Paper is one of the most important and useful materials man has ever created. Until a hundred years ago most sheets of paper in the world were made by hand, and mostly used for precious documents.

Wasps taught us how to make paper. (Have you studied a hive?) Wasps chew fibers and weeds into a kind of paste or mash, spit it out to form the walls and chambers of their hive, and when it dries it is a kind of paper sculpture.

The first people to make paper were the Chinese in 105 A.D. In the 6th century when the Chinese lost to the Arabs at the Battle of Samarkand, captured paper makers were forced to share their crafts with their new masters. A thousand years later the art of paper making reached Europe.

Paper is made from fibers
such as: weeds, bark, wood pulp, corn husks, rags, celery strings, saw-dust and wood shavings.

Fibers must be mashed, melted, reduced to pulp
by some method such as pounding, boiling, or beating. Try the easy ones such as: **corn husks, dried leaves and weeds** chopped fine.

The pulp mixed with water is called slurry.
If you dip a piece of metal window screen into the slurry and raise it up slowly and drain it, blot out the extra water and press it dry you will have a crude sheet of handmade paper.

The Quick Recycle Paper making method is the best to start with: (no chemicals, only use water.)

1. make 2 small frames (same size)
2. staple wire screen to one frame called the mold.
3. Tear up old newspaper - soak it, beat it or blend it - About one sheet of newspaper per dishpan of warm water.
4. Hold the mold, screen side up, place the empty frame on top. (The empty frame is called a DECKLE. It allows the water to drain slowly and forms the edges of the "wet-leaf")
5. Dip both frames into dish pan of slurry
6. Raise frames up slowly, and drain.
7. Remove top frame
8 & 9. Turn screen over onto paper towel blotter and sponge screen dry.
10-12. Remove screen. Put another blotter on top of "wet-leaf" and Iron dry. Remove blotters. See - you made new paper!

15

PAPER LACE HANGERS

square

1. Use a square of paper any size

2. Fold corner to corner

3 With open end down draw a ¼" Margin

4. Draw cutting lines

5. Cut in from Left side to margin on right Then cut in from right side to margin on Left etc.

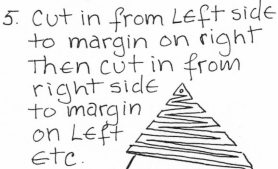

6. open folds carefully while still on table

7. Attach hanger: clip or thread and hang from high place.

16

USE: heavy paper
for big Lacy
paper
hangers.

Round

1. cut a round piece of paper.
2. Fold in half.
3. Fold in quarter.

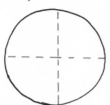

4. with open end down draw margin lines up both sides Left & right.

open end

5. Draw cutting lines and cut curves.
6. open up carefully

7. Put paper clip through center and hang from ceiling.

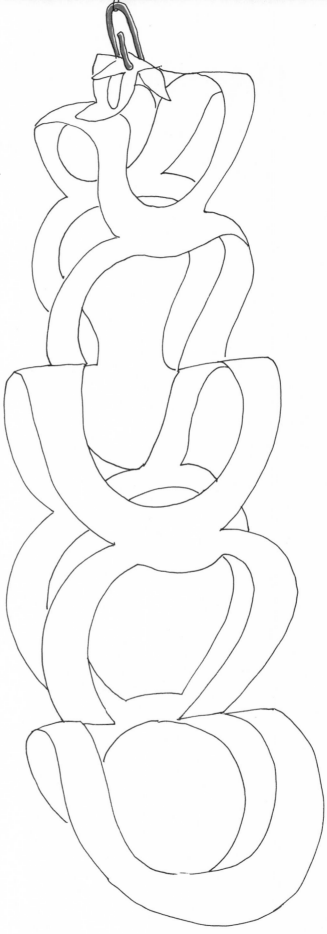

PAPER ORNAMENTS

star balls

1. Cut 7 colored paper disks.
2. Fold all but one in half.
3. Cut, with scissors, in about *halfway*.
4. slip cut disks over flat disk

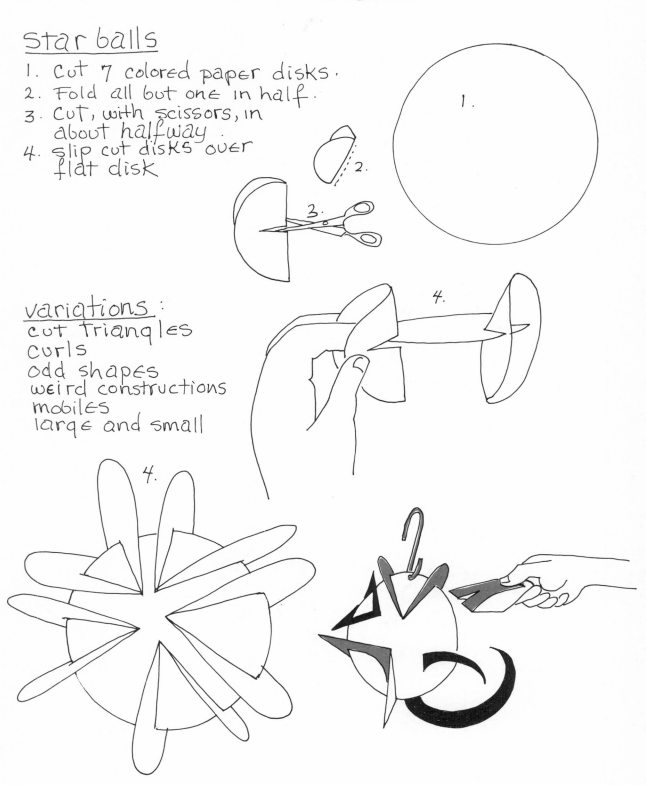

variations:
cut triangles
curls
odd shapes
weird constructions
mobiles
large and small

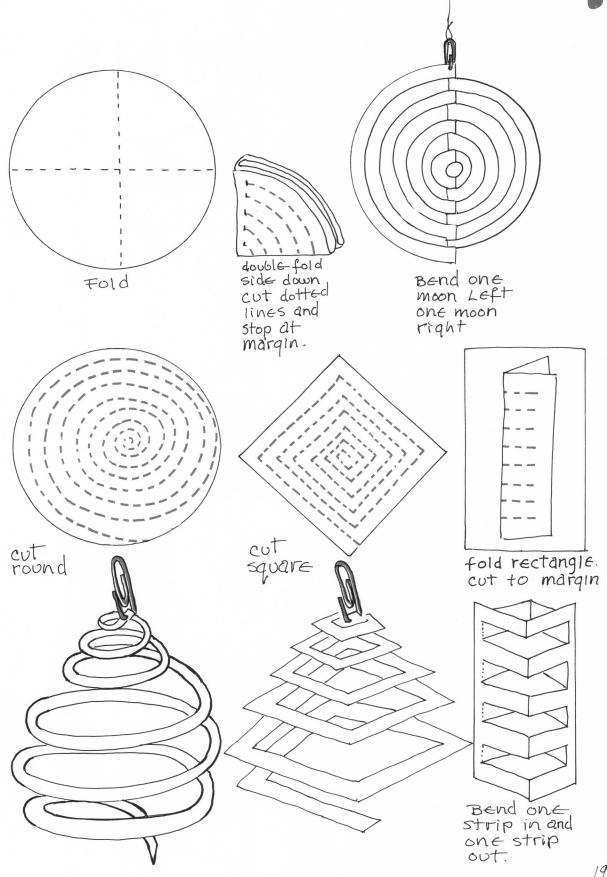

Fold

double-fold
side down
cut dotted
lines and
stop at
margin.

Bend one
moon LEFT
one moon
right

cut
round

cut
square

fold rectangle.
cut to margin

Bend one
strip in and
one strip
out.

19

PAPER CUTTING

cut and staple
tubes and funnels

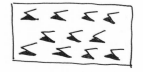
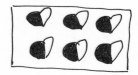

see what designs you can
make by snipping + bending
backwards

* P a P e r * Wonderful * Paper *

PAPER CONE SCULPTURE

cut and staple
or glue cones

bend
and
score
beak
and
wings

glue and
curl tail
around pencil

* Wonderful * paper * Wonder *

3-D LIFT-UP VILLAGE

Use colored construction paper

1. Draw: house, trees, pet, flowers etc.
   a city, town or village
   Leaving space between each form.

2. Cut along the drawn lines except where things bend (dotted line)

(if you don't have good sharp scissors, go over your pencil-lines with a sharp pencil until they cut through. A sheet of newspaper folded under drawing helps lead score paper.)

3. Bend shapes up so everything is standing

Good for dioramas
stage sets
christmas cards
surprises
and
· learning
about
perspective

and
City planning

FOLD & CUT

USE:
paper, cardboard or tin.
(filing cards are good)

Draw figure
on folded sheet.
note how the
fold is used
for standing
the figure up.

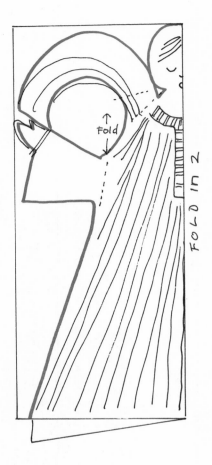

FOLD IN 2

for Standing Letters
greeting
cards
and
place
cards

FOLD IN 2.

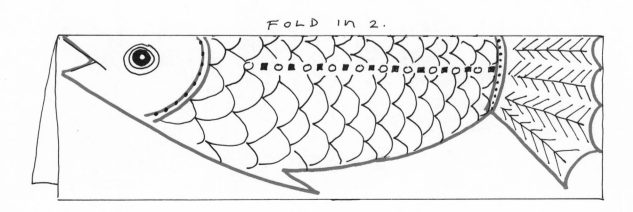

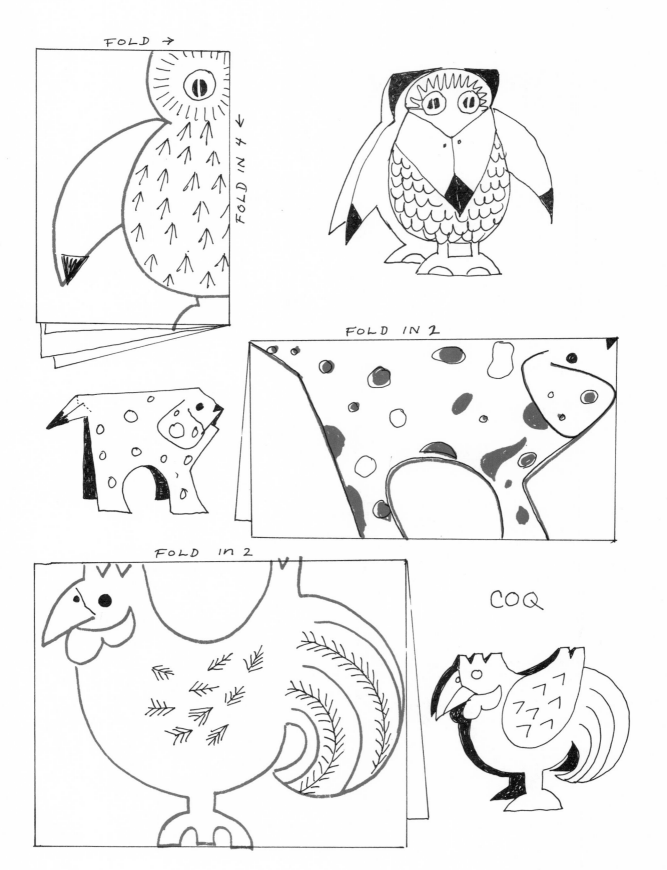

FOLD →

FOLD IN 4 ←

FOLD IN 2

FOLD IN 2

COQ

25

PAPER CURLS & MOBILES

USE: colored construction paper or oaktag. scissors pencil stapler.

cut paper strips thick and thin short and long

curl around pencil

or nail

staple big and little loops

fish mobile

snail

see what you can create. Try a butterfly.

TISSUE FISH

mobiles for
drafty places

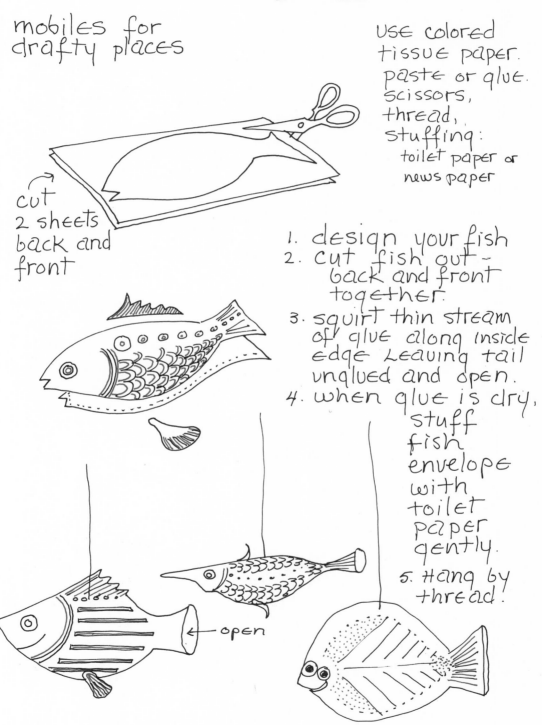

use colored
tissue paper,
paste or glue,
scissors,
thread,
stuffing:
toilet paper or
news paper

cut
2 sheets
back and
front

1. design your fish
2. cut fish out-
   back and front
   together.
3. squirt thin stream
   of glue along inside
   edge leaving tail
   unglued and open.
4. when glue is dry,
   stuff
   fish
   envelope
   with
   toilet
   paper
   gently.
5. Hang by
   thread!

← open

PAPER GLIDERS

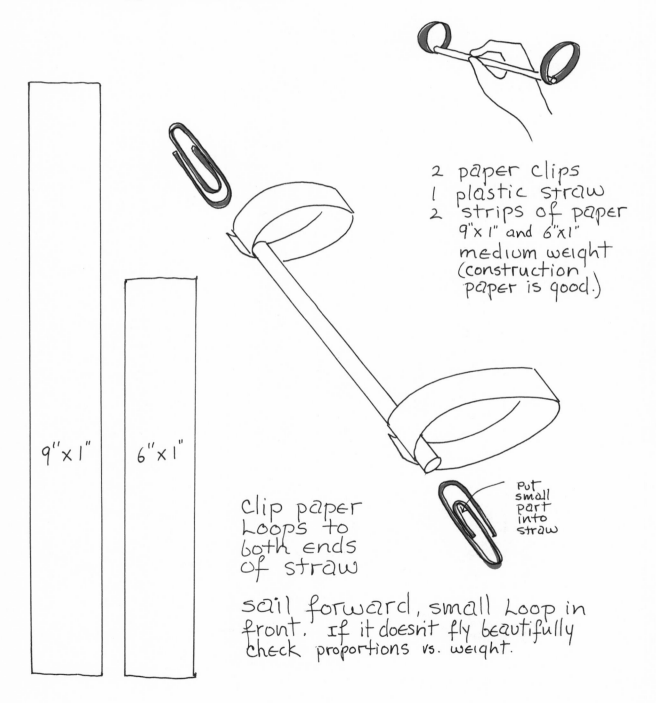

9"x1"

6"x1"

2 paper clips
1 plastic straw
2 strips of paper
9"x1" and 6"x1"
medium weight
(construction
paper is good.)

Put
small
part
into
straw

Clip paper
Loops to
both ends
of straw

sail forward, small Loop in
front. If it doesn't fly beautifully
check proportions vs. weight.

PAPER SPINNERS

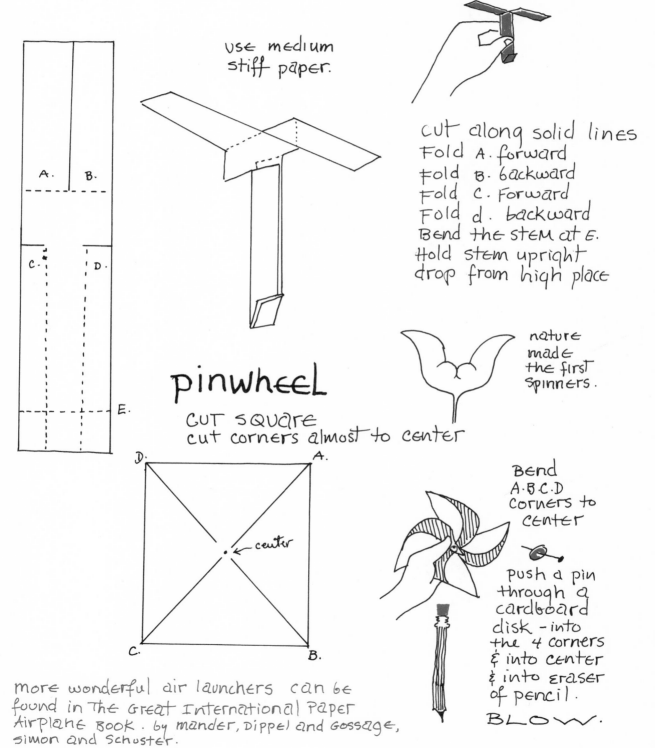

use medium stiff paper.

cut along solid lines
Fold A. forward
Fold B. backward
Fold C. forward
Fold d. backward
Bend the stem at E.
Hold stem upright
drop from high place

nature made the first spinners.

pinwheel

CUT SQUARE
cut corners almost to center

A.
B.
C.
D.
E.

D. A.
C. B.
← center

Bend A·B·C·D corners to center

push a pin through a cardboard disk - into the 4 corners & into center & into eraser of pencil.

BLOW.

more wonderful air launchers can be found in The Great International Paper Airplane Book. by Mander, Dippel and Gossage, Simon and Schuster.

PAPER FACES

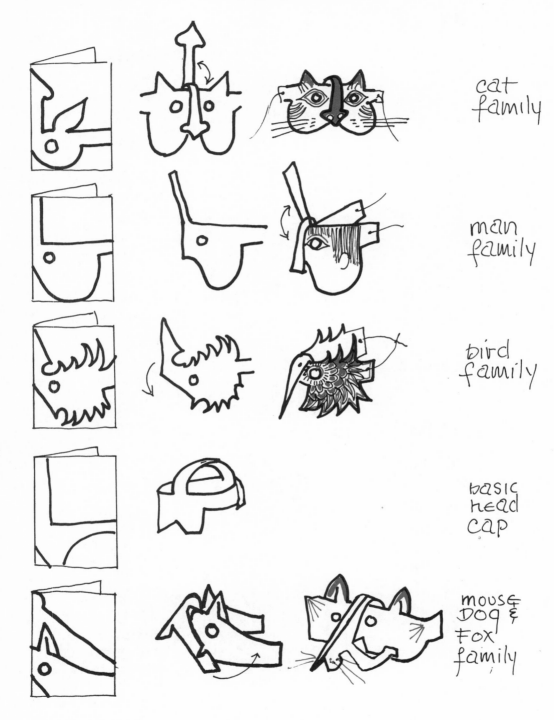

cat
family

man
family

bird
family

basic
head
cap

mouse
Dog &
Fox
family

color nose on back
of paper & fold
forward.
↓

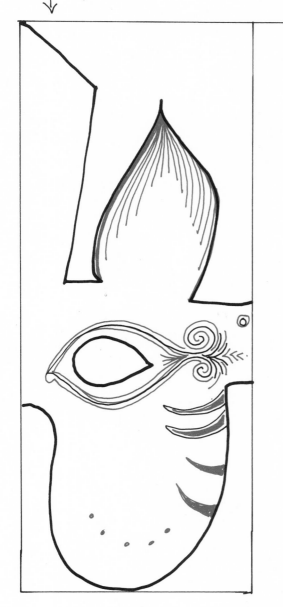

basic mask
actual size
eye & nose
placement
good for
adult or
child.

experiment
with
typewriter
sheets
until you
develop
some good
designs

fold Lengthwise

∧ Ω ◊ ∧ ↑

choose ear shape

◊ ψ ◊ V

choose nose shape

Michael grater has made a real science of
paper faces . published by Taplinger.

F INGER PUPPETS

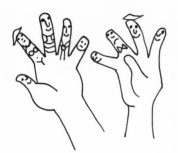

During a long automobile trip when we were children, a friend of my parents rode in the back seat with all the squabbling kids. She drew faces on her fingers and told us stories all the way. It was a wonderful trip and we forgot to thank her.

Fingers fantastic fingers.

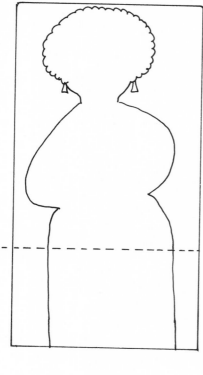

Fold
finger
section
back-
wards

USE
Filing cards
or stiff paper
1. Draw your puppet.
2. Cut out figure.
3. Cut holes to fit
   YOUR fingers.
4. Fold finger section
   backwards.
5. Put fingers through
   holes. Let fingers dance.

cut out

to fit you

PAPER BAG PUPPETS

Don't throw away
your lunch bag
draw a puppet
on it.

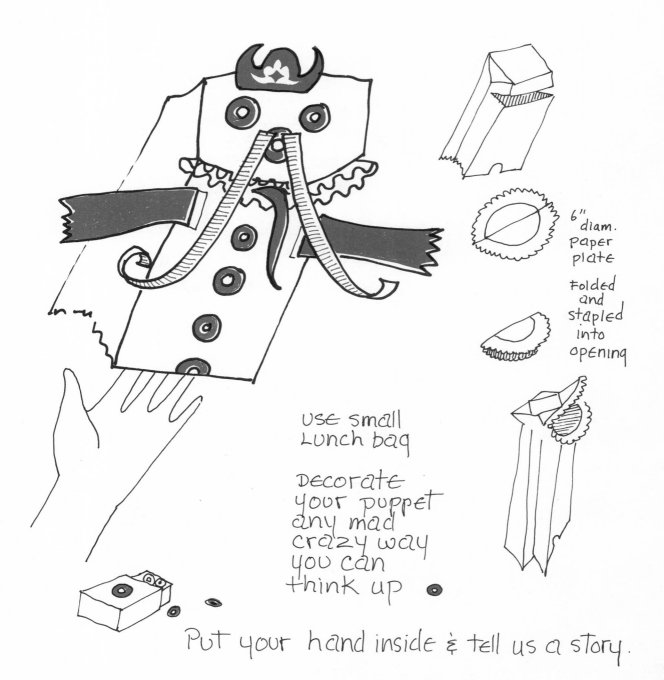

6" diam. paper plate

Folded and stapled into opening

use small Lunch bag

Decorate your puppet any mad crazy way you can think up

Put your hand inside & tell us a story.

CORRUGATED CUT-AWAY

Design boards
for older children

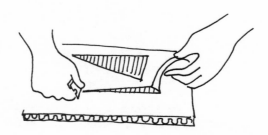

Use a cardboard grocery box
cut out the flat good sides.

If there is a choice
use the thin side (wall).

with a mat or Exacto knife
or single edged razor blade
cut into thin wall (not too deep)

Lift the thin wall up
off the corrugated humps

The trick is to coax
the peel off one
hump at a time.

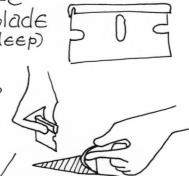

If wall is heavily glued
choose a less sturdy
box.

Razor blades are too dangerous for little kids. For safety
use one edged blades or tape one edge of a 2 sided blade.

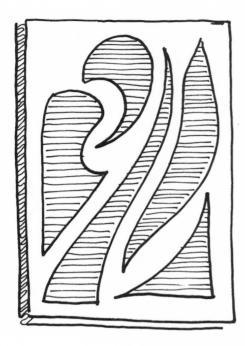

make simple shapes
(wiggles and curls
are difficult to cut).

not only
are they
decorative
as is.

you can also
make prints
from them:

roll them with
Lino ink.
press paper on
inked surface
and peel off
a print or 10, 25 maybe

37

PRINTING

FINGERS

PRINTING VEGETABLES

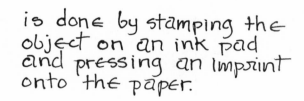

is done by stamping the object on an ink pad and pressing an imprint onto the paper.

or spreading the ink on an object or relief surface from which one can pull off many prints.

you can print:

Fingers
objects
fruits
vegetables

Piet one day old

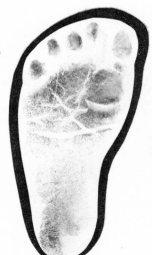

40

APPLE

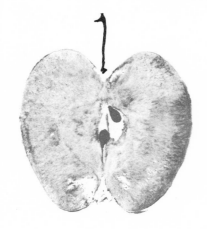

BANANA STALK
BANANA STALK
BANANA STALK
BANANA STALK

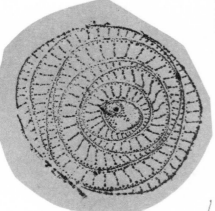

STRING BEAN

ONION

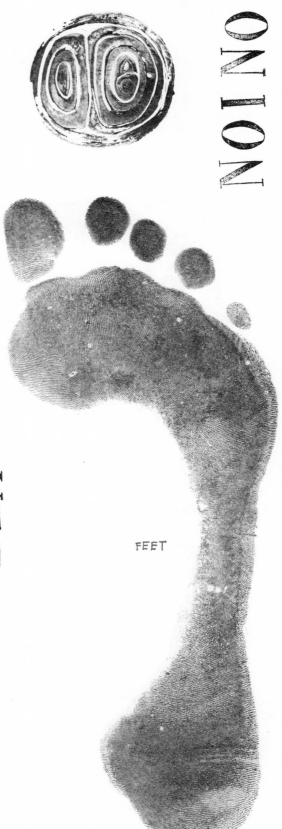

FEET

shapes can be cut from potatoes
carrots, turnips & parsnips —
pressed in a stamp-pad.

42

This owl business was all made from these simple shapes – put together.

ROLLER PRINTING

can be done with any cylinder
that has been inked or painted
or pressed on a wet stamp pad and rolled out on paper.

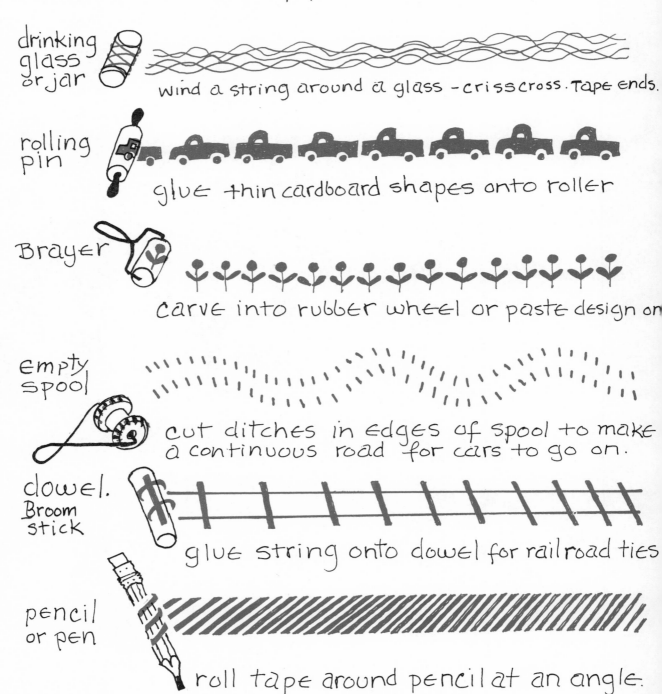

drinking glass or jar

wind a string around a glass - crisscross. Tape ends.

rolling pin

glue thin cardboard shapes onto roller

Brayer

carve into rubber wheel or paste design on

empty spool

cut ditches in edges of spool to make a continuous road for cars to go on.

dowel. Broom stick

glue string onto dowel for railroad ties

pencil or pen

roll tape around pencil at an angle.

44

PRINTING POTATOES

Potato printing is by far the easiest, most practical economical printing method, especially for small people who shouldn't use knives.

Potatoes · Knife · paper · paint.

For pre-schoolers and handicapped children, pre-cut a collection of shapes to be used as stampers.

for printing
use:
Stamp pads
Tempera in dishes
or water-soluble
Linoleum ink.

See what you can make out of these basic shapes. Tack up a big piece of wrapping paper. **Print.**

Remember: recognizable form is not what interests little kids at first. They just want to see what happens!

BLOCK PRINTING

1. Wood — — — — — — — — — designs etched and cut from wood surface with Linoleum tools

2. Linoleum — — — — — — — comes mounted on wooden blocks or in sheets, easily carved and etched with Lino tools.

3. Plaster — — — — — — — made in flat plaques which can be scratched and printed.

4. Styrofoam — — — — — — Draw or scratch — no knife ... GREAT for little kids. just use a pencil, pen or paperclip.

5. Corrugated — — — — — cut-away: negative relief no cost and very interesting.

6. String relief — — — — raised line: string glued to any surface like cardboard. Easily printed

7. Collage relief — — — raised form: cardboard or inner tire tubes cut and glued to cardboard

8. Scratch board — — gesso surface, scratching and graffiti line drawing.

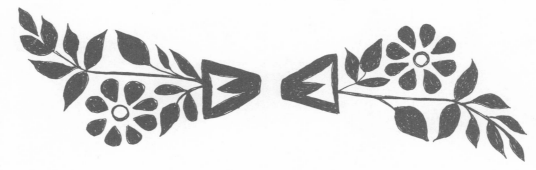

All of these materials make good prints.
and all can be printed in the following way:
Block printing ink can be
oil base or water base.

start with water base-it is easier to clean.

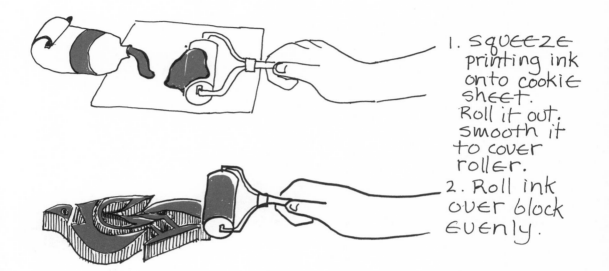

1. SQUEEZE
printing ink
onto cookie
sheet.
Roll it out.
smooth it
to cover
roller.

2. Roll ink
over block
evenly.

3. To Print:
Press inked block onto paper
or press paper onto inked
block. Rub gently. Peel paper
back

"give me a fish
and I eat
for a day

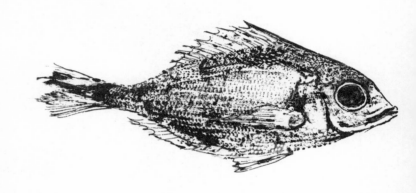

teach me to fish
and I eat
for a lifetime "

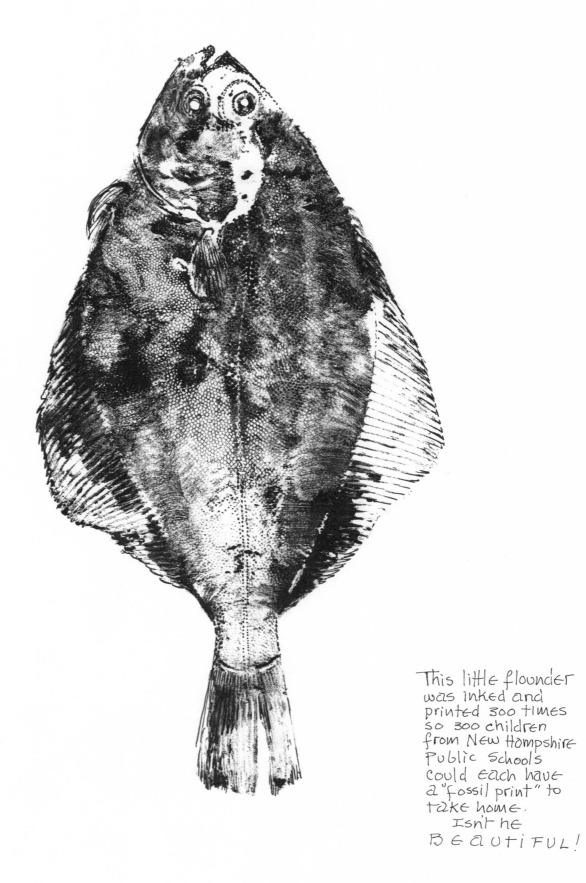

This little flounder
was inked and
printed 300 times
so 300 children
from New Hampshire
Public Schools
could each have
a "fossil print" to
take home.
Isn't he
BEAUTIFUL!

FINGER PAINTING

finger paints come ready made
or you can make your own
But Chocolate Pudding is the most fun
and you can lick your fingers. !

Quick and inexpensive Finger Paint Recipes:

A.	B.
1. cup cornstarch diluted 1 quart boiling water ½ cup soap flakes	1 cup warm water ¼ cup flour. whip it up and add powder color

OR INSTANT

Chocolate Pudding : mix as directed on pack
 or a little on the gushy side

messing about: if you want to KEEP designs,
 use slippery shelf paper.

Printing : Put paint or pudding on a tray.
1. make your design in the paint.
2. With clean hands, gently lay a
 piece of paper on wet design.
3. Press very very lightly over surface.
4. Pull print up slowly. Allow to dry.

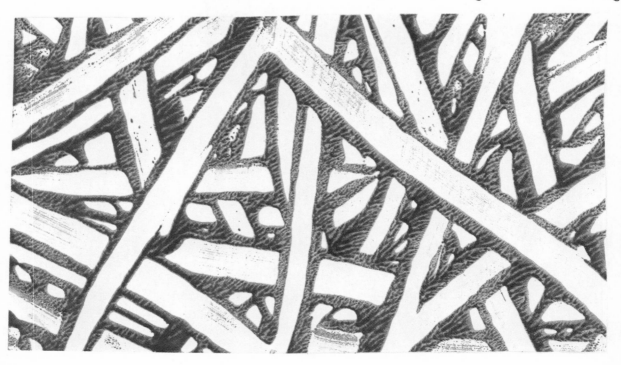

CHOCOLATE · PUDDING · PRINTS

PAINTING for beginners

before you look for "talent" or recognizable form, enjoy the sweeping of liquid around a clean sheet of paper. — For someone who has never done it before it symbolizes all childhood taboos:

MAKING A MESS · SPILLING · DRIPPING · SMEARING · SCRUBBING a real "Mud-Luscious" activity couched in PERMISSION!

1st adventure : "MESSING ABOUT" with the primary colors: RED, YELLOW & BLUE, with a dry brush and a wet brush.

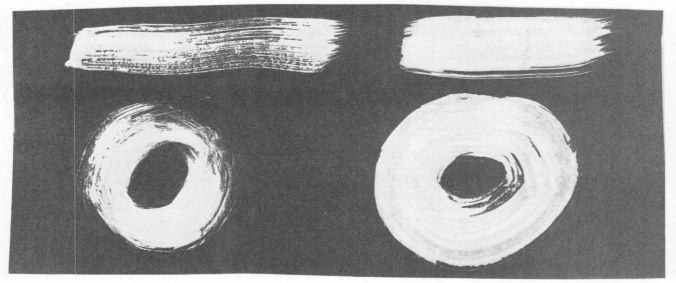

<u>2nd adventure:</u> MiXiNG Colors, endless combinations
can all be made from RED, YELLOW & BLUE
Make: oranges   browns
greens   tans
purples   blacks
Have a color mixing contest. Make a color wheel

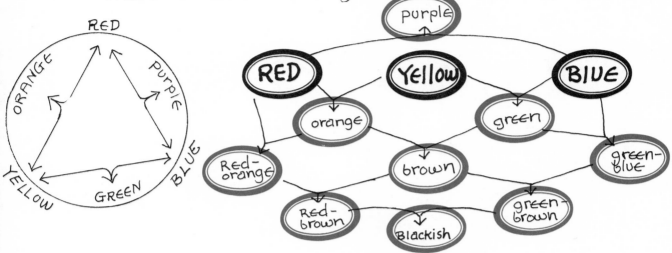

<u>3rd Adventure:</u> Controlled DESIGNS
paint an outline design with one color
fill in with other colors

<u>4th ADVENTURE:</u> Action · MOTION · RHYTHM
paint to music   paint a drum beat
paint a mood   paint sad
paint warm   paint happy
paint cold   paint as you wish....

From here on you know the tools, materials and what
they will do. Feel free to experiment - Discover and
DEVELOP your own originality, skill, to express yourself
and tell your own story.

<u>Parents and Teachers:</u> don't limit your approval -
CONSIDER: control   Mood   invention
form   texture   perspective
space   skill   solutions
Contour   Self-expression pleasure
freedom   joy   fun

WINDOW SHADE
MAPS & MURALS

USE :

Old white window shades
or new ones (5 & 10 & Hardware stores).
Attach the holding fixture
to a wall so shades can be
easily changeable.

Draw or Paint
a new horizon
an abstract design
a sunny garden
a summer dream
a map
a friend

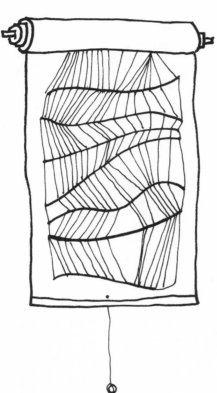

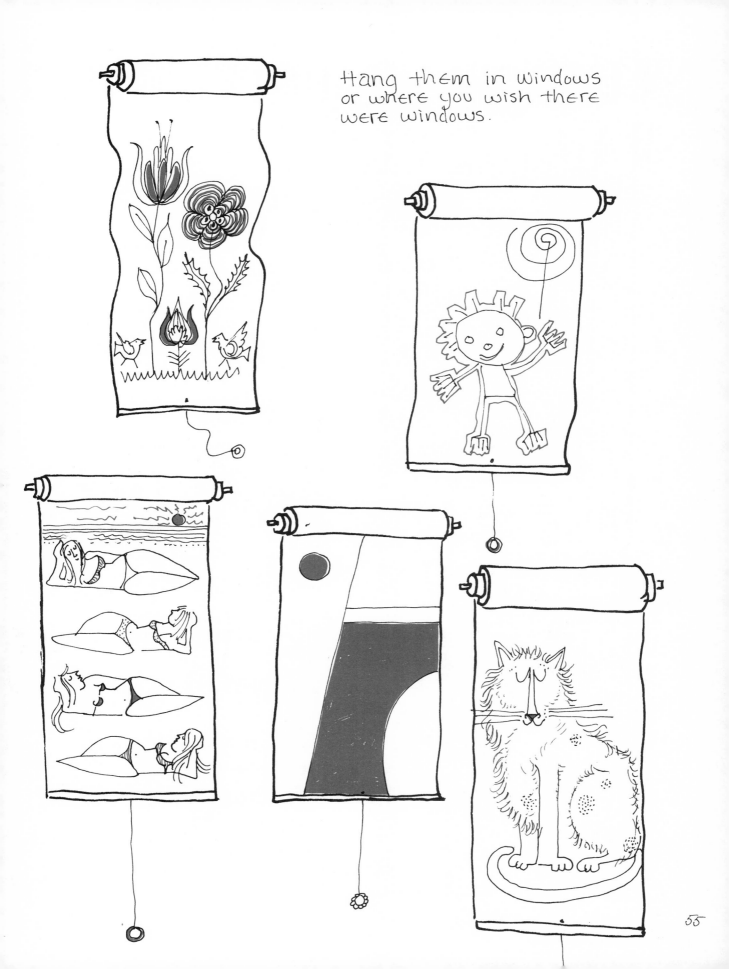

Hang them in windows
or where you wish there
were windows.

CRAYONS for all ages

A. Sgraffito scratch boards

1. Cover a piece of paper with strong colors
2. Color over the colors with solid black crayon (or india ink or poster tempera black mixed with detergent to make it stick – 1 tsp. black to 4 soap)
3. Scratch with paper clip, nail, ball point etc. into the wax exposing the colors below.

B. Crayon "stained glass"
(oil transparencies)

1. Paint a picture with India ink black
2. Color design with crayons
3. Turn picture over Dab rag in veg. oil and rub it over back of picture to make it transparent
4. Towel off excess
5. Tape "stained glass" transparencies onto windows

crayons were made for drawing and coloring. The best way to use them is to peal off the paper and break crayon in two pieces. (They will break anyway so you may as well have the fun of doing it on <u>purpose</u> !) use them every which-way.

C. crayon rubbings

1. remove paper from crayon
2. place thin sheet of paper over object.
3. rub side of crayon over surface.

Try : coins, fossils, dishes with raised patterns, man hole covers, tomb stones brass bas reliefs, shells, dry scaly fish, keys and hundreds of other objects.

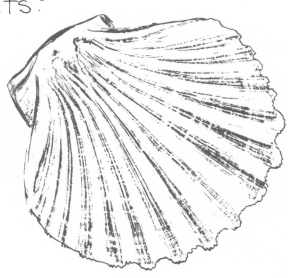

Make a white crayon rubbing and paint it over with india ink or ebony stain.

D. crayon wax resist batik

1. <u>Dry resist</u> : draw crayon picture on old bed sheet. Iron between newspapers.
2. <u>Melted wax wet resist</u> : melt crayons in a muffin tin on hot plate or food warmer. Paint on old bed sheet. Iron wax out between newspaper.

SLOTTED ANIMALS

no nails.
collapsible
interchangeable

cut models out of light
weight cardboard

Then make big ones, to
climb on, out of wood.

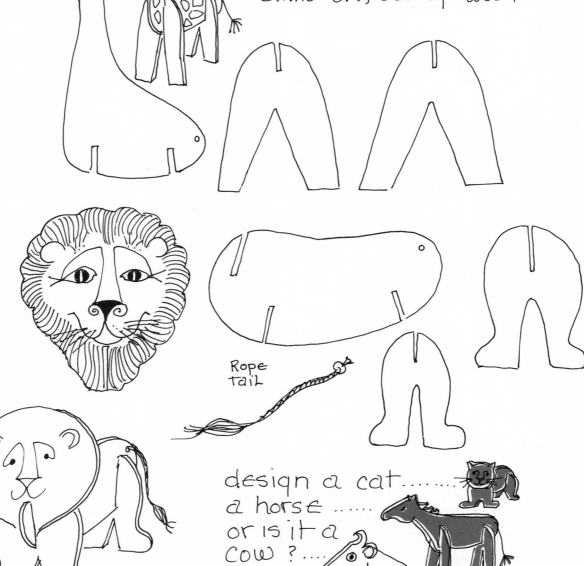

Rope
Tail

design a cat........
a horse .....
or is it a
cow ?.....

58

KIKO'S SEAGULL
and other birds

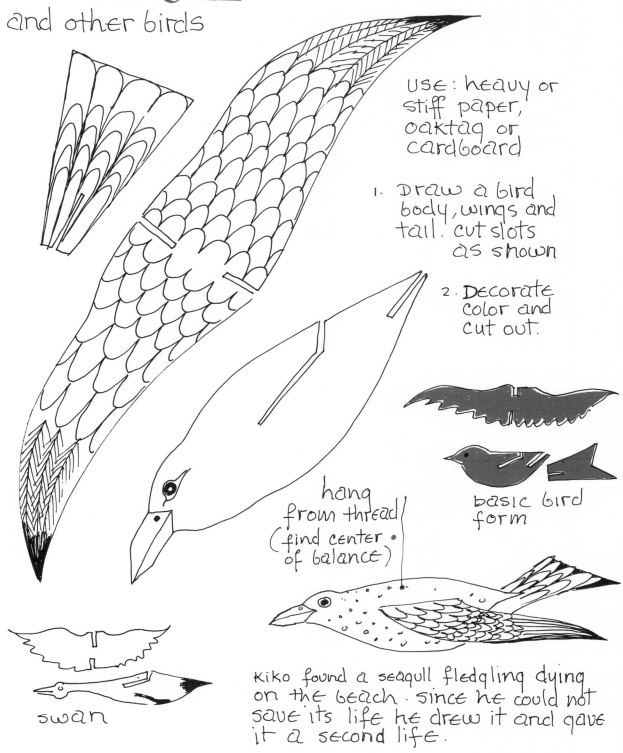

USE: heavy or stiff paper, oaktag or cardboard

1. Draw a bird body, wings and tail. Cut slots as shown

2. Decorate color and cut out.

hang from thread (find center of balance)

basic bird form

swan

Kiko found a seagull fledgling dying on the beach. Since he could not save its life he drew it and gave it a second life.

BED FRIENDS & UMMM-DEARS

Use a nice soft old undershirt or unbleached muslin.

1. Draw a friend with an indelible pen or felt marker

2. cut it out double

3. turn inside out, sew 2 sides together leaving about 3" open on one side so you can stuff your doll with old stockings.

4. turn doll right side out. stuff and sew closed.

PILLOW COZIES

Draw a big cozy puppy on your pillow case

use crayons (press hard)
outline with indelible felt marker
Put a thick pack of newspaper inside
pillow case and one sheet of paper
towel on top of your crayon drawing
and iron it until all the wax melts
out into the paper towels, leaving the
drawing permanently printed on the pillow case.
you can make 4 cozies and change them
every week

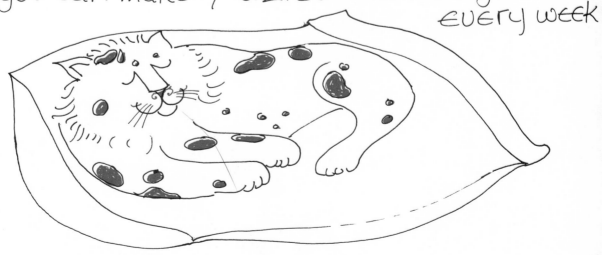

wash gently in warm water.

APPLIQUÉ & STITCHERY

USE: cotton scraps and old clothes
1. cut out simple designs of one color
   and sew them onto another color
   turning the edges under as you go

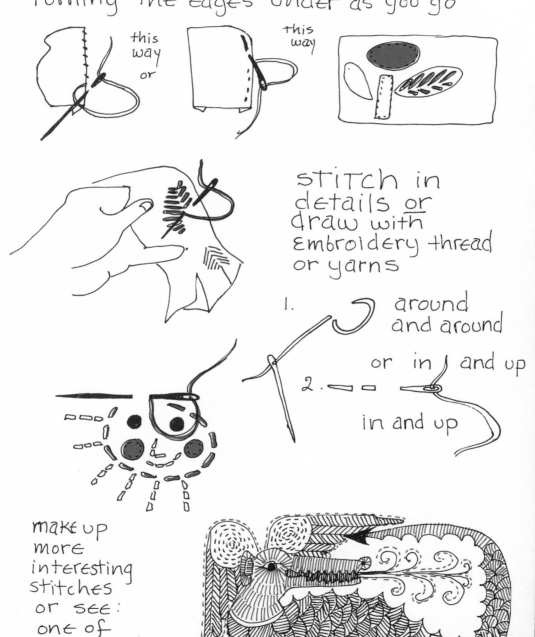

this way or

this way

stitch in
details or
draw with
embroidery thread
or yarns

1. around
   and around

   or in and up

2. in and up

make up
more
interesting
stitches
or see:
one of
many good
stitchery
books.

Cut-away Applique

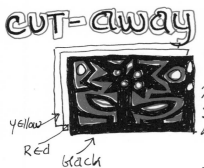

yellow
Red
black

1. Cut Red, yellow and black cotton fabric about 9x12 making 3 layers the same size. Put black on Top.
2. Baste the 3 layers together at edges.
3. Draw with pencil or chalk on black layer.
4. Cut through black to expose red layer. Turn edges under and sew down
5. Cut through red to expose yellow layer leaving fat red margins. Turn edges and sew.

The San Blas Islanders make a real art of this.

PORTABLE HOUSES

4 PIECE A-FRAME
plywood or cardboard

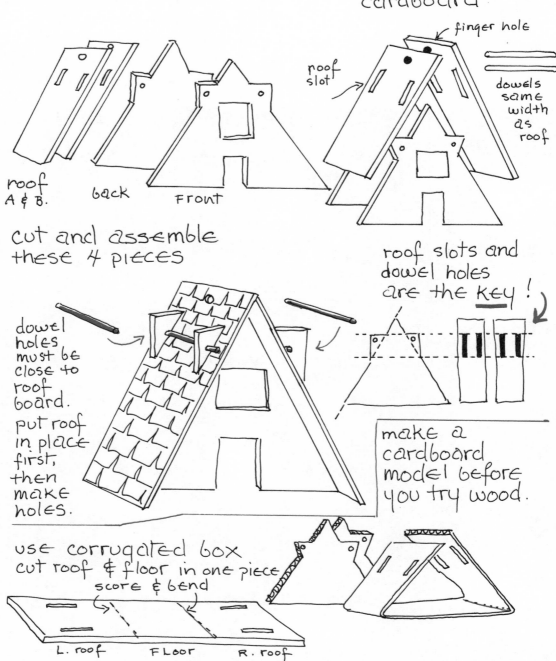

finger hole

roof slot

dowels same width as roof

roof A & B.

back

Front

cut and assemble these 4 pieces

roof slots and dowel holes are the **KEY**!

dowel holes must be close to roof board.

put roof in place first, then make holes.

make a cardboard model before you try wood.

use corrugated box
cut roof & floor in one piece
score & bend

L. roof   FLOOR   R. roof

BOX HOUSES

Use big or small corrugated grocery box.

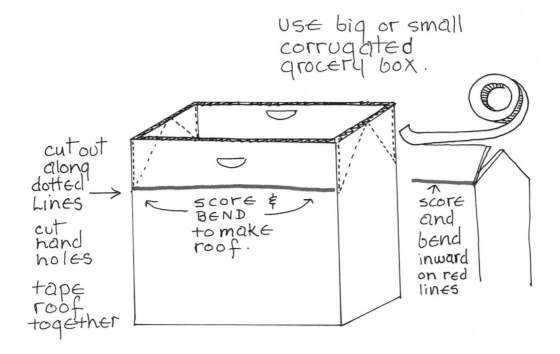

cut out along dotted lines →

cut hand holes

tape roof together

score & BEND to make roof.

score and bend inward on red lines

La Mia

you can make a house to sit in! use a refrigerator or freezer box.

From quiet homes and first beginnings
Out to the undiscovered ends,
There's nothing worth the wear of winning,
But laughter and the love of friends.   Hilaire Belloc.

PIET'S HORSE BENCH

collapsible · portable ·
designed for my son Piet
when he was 4

F.A.O. schwarz in N.Y.C.
made them for their
christmas catalogue
several years ago.

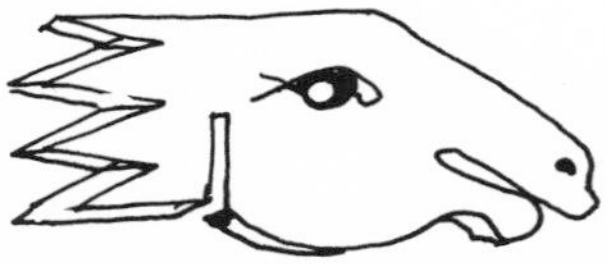

I made this sturdy little bench
in many sizes out of pine
boards with a coping saw,
a drill, sandpaper and an
indelible felt marker.

It has no
nails. It is
pegged
together
with ¾"
dowels, and a
slotted head.

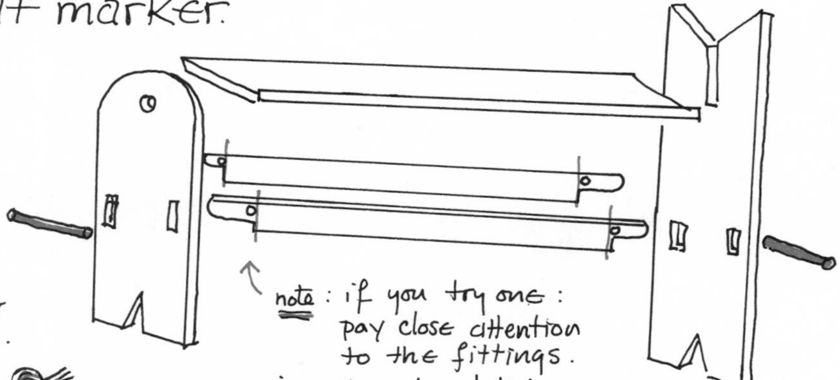

and a rope tail

note: if you try one:
pay close attention
to the fittings.
i.e. The dowel holes

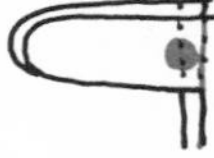

must be
up close to the
tail and head board
or bench will rock

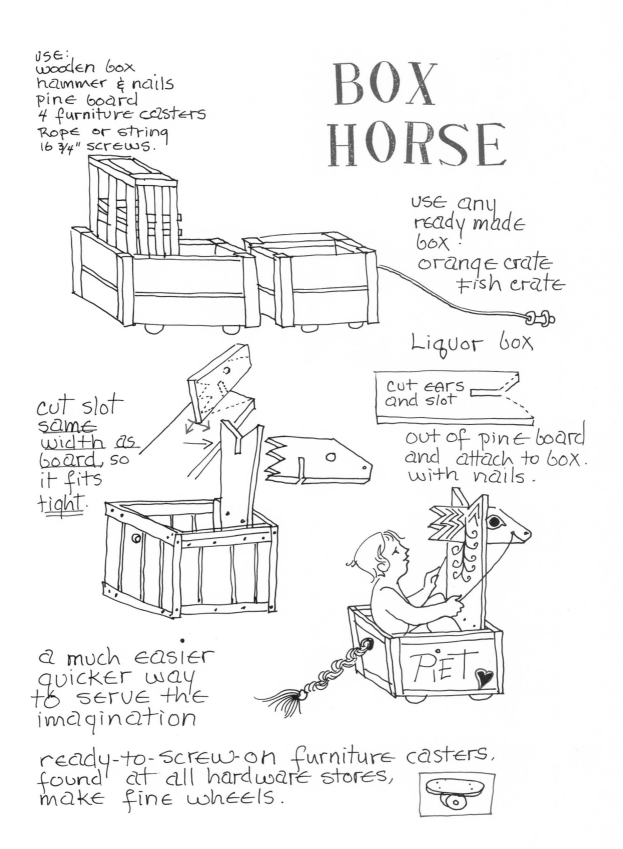

USE:
wooden box
hammer & nails
pine board
4 furniture casters
Rope or string
16 3/4" screws.

BOX HORSE

use any
ready made
box!
orange crate
fish crate

Liquor box

cut ears
and slot

out of pine board
and attach to box.
with nails.

cut slot
same
width as
board, so
it fits
tight.

a much easier
quicker way
to serve the
imagination

ready-to-screw-on furniture casters,
found at all hardware stores,
make fine wheels.

PiET

Macdougal street
SKATE SKOOTER

every boy who played in the streets of new York City when I was growing up rode a skate skooter made out of an orange crate and a roller skate.

a can of paint to make it fierce

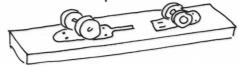

split a roller skate, remove shoe grips and ankle straps Nail one section at either end of skooter.

" You've got to steer by anticipation "
Buckminster Fuller.

GO-CARS

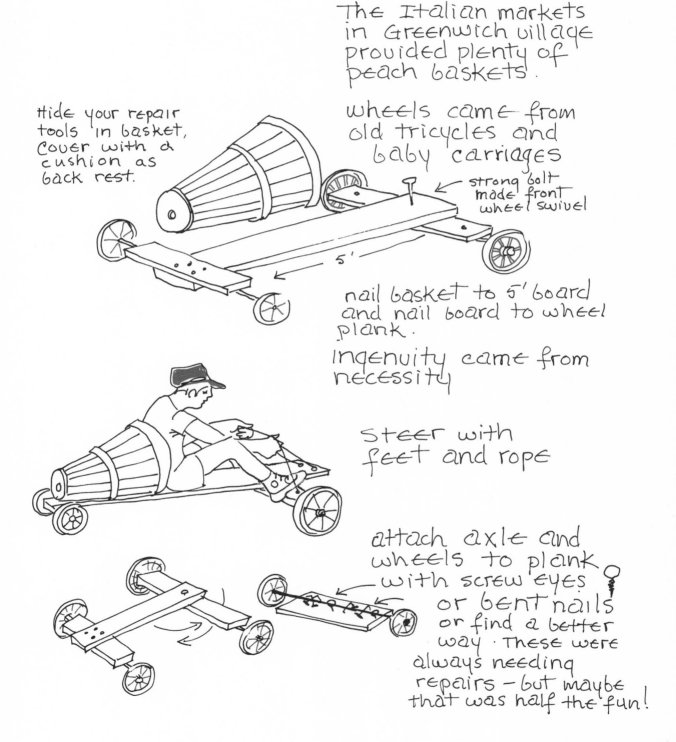

The Italian markets in Greenwich village provided plenty of peach baskets.

Hide your repair tools in basket, cover with a cushion as back rest.

Wheels came from old tricycles and baby carriages

strong bolt made front wheel swivel

5'

nail basket to 5' board and nail board to wheel plank.

Ingenuity came from necessity

steer with feet and rope

attach axle and wheels to plank with screw eyes or bent nails or find a better way. These were always needing repairs — but maybe that was half the fun!

STILTS

Stilts are used to raise men
off the flooded ground
to reach fruits on tall trees
to see over high fences
to look like a giant in the circus
or just to make you feel BIG and Tall.

I'll never forget Sam Warren
who made me my first pair of stilts
and raised them from low to high
as I gained confidence. He was
kind to children. Someone must
have been kind to him and he
passed it on.

MAKE TWO:
1. USE 2" diam. posts
   or 1" x 1½" wood strips
   6' long depending on how big you are.
2. Sandpaper the poles smooth
3. Cut foot blocks 6" x 4" x 1½"
4. Decide on
   height of foot
   block from
   the ground
   (start low!)

$\uparrow$ 4"
6"
$\downarrow$ 1½"

} = 2 foot blocks.

5. Drill foot block holes
6. USE 2½" or 2" screws

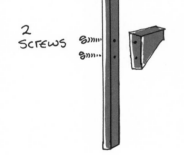

2 SCREWS

Action:
a. stand on a step or box
   to get started
b. put stilt poles under your arms
c. climb onto the foot blocks
d. walk forward by shifting
   your weight from one foot
   to the other, holding the
   foot blocks up tightly against
   your feet.

(if starting and balancing is
hard, lean against a wall or
ask a friend to hold you
until you get the feel of it.)

Tin can
easy foot risers

USE BIG TOMATO cans, bottom end up.
POKE holes
for strings.
stand on cans.
Hold strings tight
and WALK . . . .

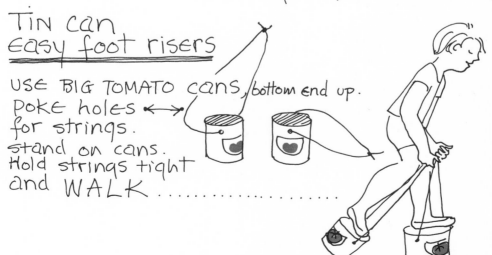

GRANDFATHER'S WILLOW WHISTLE

In the days when pocket knives were for whittling and mumblety-peg my dear grandfather showed us how to make willow whistles. (He also gave us to understand that dispite upheavals and world calamity life would go on and there was time for children to grow and think and WONDER....)

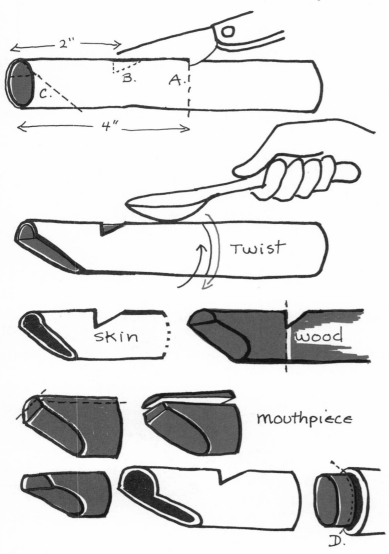

In the spring when the sap runs cut 6" of willow twig.

1. Cut through the skin at A. (not the wood.) Cut air hole B. through wood Cut mouthpiece C. "
2. Rub stick with the bowl of a spoon until juice runs and you can twist the skin off of the wood.
3. Slide skin from stick carefully.
4. Cut off mouthpiece from wooden part.
5. note angle and cut or rub mouthpiece on sandpaper until you have removed the proper amount of wood to make this angle.
6. slide mouthpiece back into skin.
7. Cut stick at A. and make a plug about 1/4" to fit inside whistle skin at bottom D.
8. BLOW

72

POCKET WONDERS

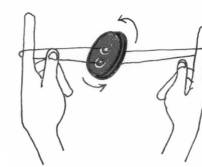

BUTTON SPINNER

half- or small cork

CORK COPTER

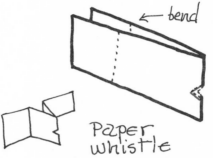

← bend

cut ◄ at edge of fold

paper whistle

card-board disk and toothpick

SPINNING TOP

elastic band

tooth pick

walking SPOOL

Tighten by twisting elastic. Let it go on the floor

clothes pin butterfly

IMPROVISED EMERGENCY HAMMER

USE: A sturdy branch of wood
about 8" long × 1" diameter
A Big bolt with nut,
thong and nail

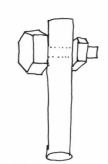

Depending on your
available tools
make model A. or B.

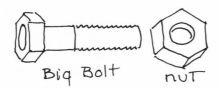

Big Bolt   nut

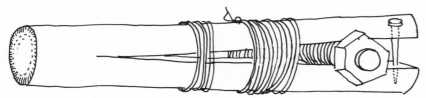

Split branch model
Split branch ¾ of the
way down. Set bolt
in place about 1" from
end. Lash fore and aft
with thong or use screw
to hold top and bottom fast

B. Drilled hole model
Drill hole for boltshaft
put shaft through hole.
screw nut tight

To make
one end
good for
pulling nails
File a V wedge
at end of bolt
shaft and allow
to protrude ½ an inch.

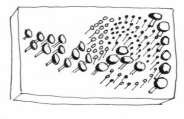

MAKE:
A house
A bookcase
A toy or
A nail-head
mosaic in
a block of
wood.

note:
This and many other ingenious improvised tools have been
developed by clever people at The Education Development Center
for use in Africa.

THE LITTLE HACK SAW BLADE

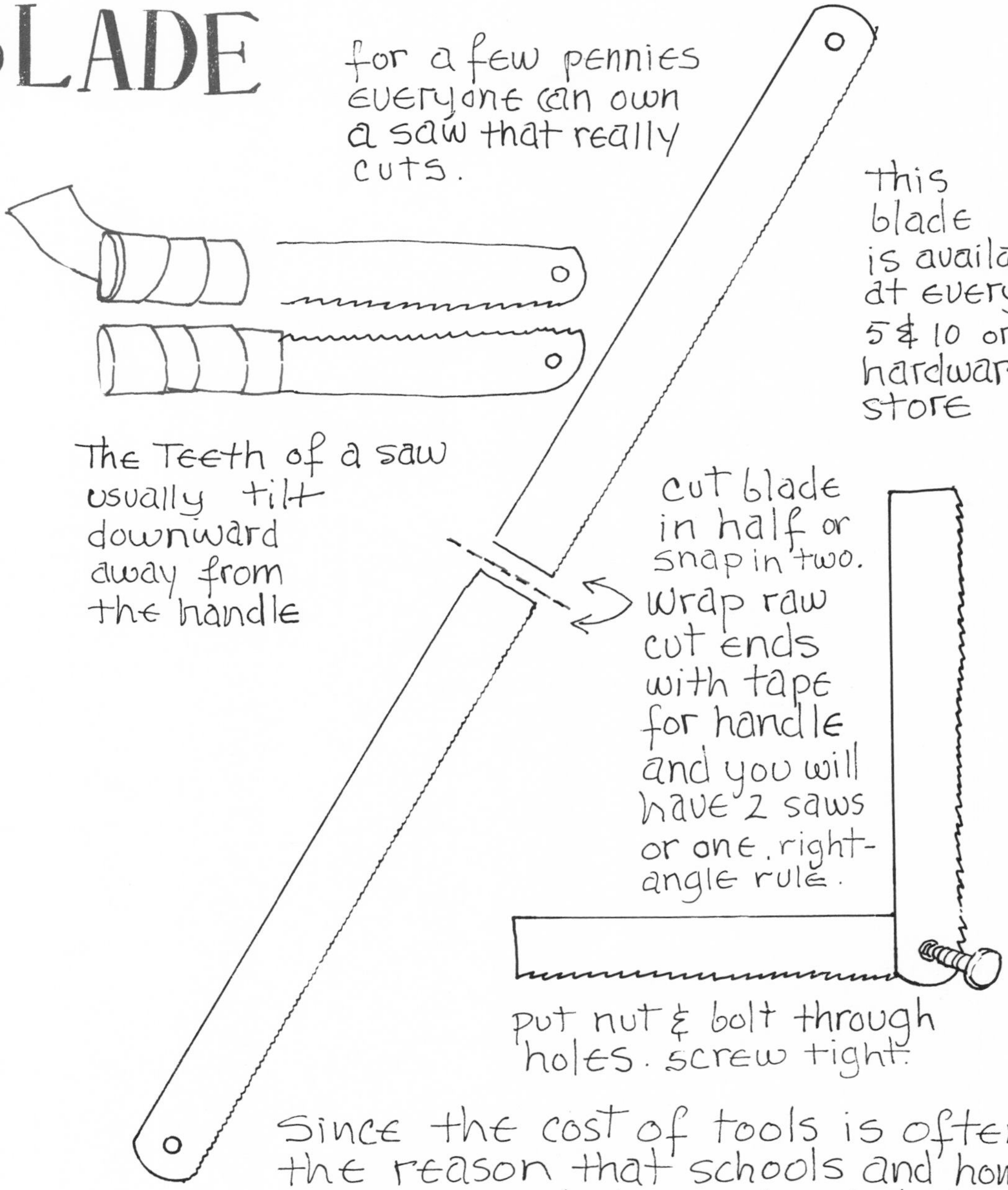

for a few pennies
everyone can own
a saw that really
cuts.

this
blade
is available
at every
5 & 10 or
hardware
store

The teeth of a saw
usually tilt
downward
away from
the handle

cut blade
in half or
snap in two.
Wrap raw
cut ends
with tape
for handle
and you will
have 2 saws
or one right-
angle rule.

put nut & bolt through
holes. screw tight.

Since the cost of tools is often
the reason that schools and homes
have no workshops. The Workshop for
Learning things in Watertown helps
teachers figure out ways to adapt and
improvise so everyone can have his own
workshop.

ALASKAN BOW DRILL

(similar drills are still used in primitive cultures for sparking fires as well as for drilling holes)

USE: A green twig for bow
       A stone or block of wood palm piece with indentation to hold shaft
       A 4" x ¾" straight branch for shaft
       A thong or gut string long enough to hold bow bent.
       A bit of flint or sharpened steel rod.

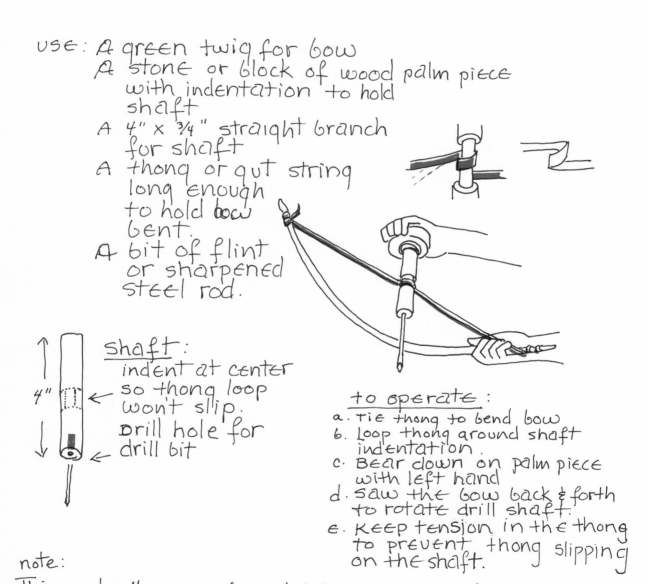

shaft:
indent at center so thong loop won't slip.
Drill hole for drill bit

4" ←

to operate:
a. Tie thong to bend bow
b. Loop thong around shaft indentation.
c. Bear down on palm piece with left hand
d. saw the bow back & forth to rotate drill shaft.
e. keep tension in the thong to prevent thong slipping on the shaft.

note:
This and other marvelous drills can be found in Drills from Simple Working Models of Historic Machines by Aubrey F. Burstall. Edward Arnold, London.

COAT HANGER BOW DRILL

Developed by the EDC Design Lab. for use with its social studies program, "Man : a course of study." Available in the Netsilik Eskimo MATCH unit on loan from the Boston Children's Museum.

MAKE YOUR OWN!

Cut dowel. drill hole in bottom for a case-hardened steel flooring nail. Glue nail in place and sharpen point. Find a block of wood or indented stone to hold drill rod straight.

Put object to be drilled in vise or hole in the ground

coat hanger (wood)

remove hook drill holes for thong. Tie knot at ends of thong to keep it in hanger bow.

rib bone bow

from a cow will work as well as the caribou used by the Netsilik Eskimo, in making soap stone and seal tusk carvings.

Use sawing motion back and forth

GRASS HATS & MATS

Grasses and weeds
bound with sinew, strips of bark
or vine strings, allowed man
to make mats to protect him
from the damp cold earth, hats to
cover his head from the sun,
containers to carry things and
rock babies in.

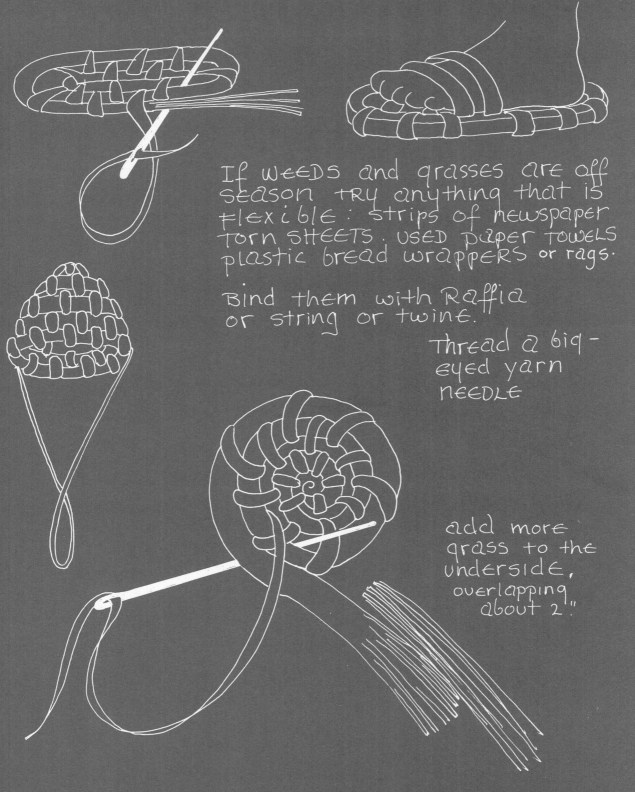

If WEEDS and grasses are off
season try anything that is
FLEXIbLE: strips of newspaper
torn SHEETS. USED paper towels
plastic bread WRAPPERS or rags.

Bind them with Raffia
or string or twine.

Thread a big-
eyed yarn
NEEDLE

add more
grass to the
UNDERSIDE,
overlapping
about 2"

SOLES FOR THE FEET

LEAF SKELETONS

oak LEAVES
are good.

choose your favorite
green leaf

1. on a folded towel or
   a carpet scrap,
   pound your leaf
   with a hairbrush
   or scrub brush gently.

2. pound about 5 minutes
   until the center
   green part of leaf
   is lacy and veins
   are exposed.

3. To preserve —
   iron between sheets
   of wax paper.
   Or mount between
   2 pieces of window
   glass, as shown
   in the weed
   Keeper.

First
you need
patience

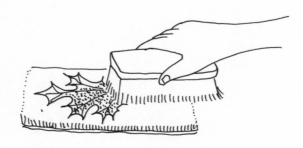

WEED KEEPER

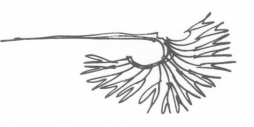

choose flat things
that press well.

The
trick
to using
a glass
cutter
is to
make
one
sure
clean
stroke
forward
or
backward
but not
both.
Do not
rock
or
bear
down
too
hard
or
too
lightly.
PRACTICE!

buy or
1. cut 2
  pieces of
  glass the
  same size.

2. Find a lovely
   weed or
   flower.

3. Press it
   between pieces
   of glass.

4. Tuck a paperclip
   or bent wire loop
   between glass
   to serve as a hanger.

5. Use epoxy glue
   around edges of
   glass to hold them
   together. Black epoxy looks
   like lead.

P.S. Plexiglas
or heavy
acetate
can be used
in place of
glass.
And bits of
colored tissue
designs in
place of
nature.
And tape glass
together in
place of glue.

ANIMATED MOTION

MOVIES
what a
fantastic
idea!

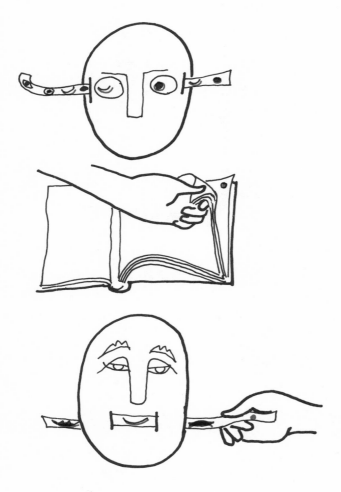

you can pull
a filmstrip
of eyeballs
through a mask
and animate
a still face.

I can draw
a red dot on
every page of
this book and you can
see the dot dance
by snapping the
corners.

you can open
and close
a conversation
and smile
and frown

you can learn a lot about sequence
and motion by making snap and spin
movies.

MOVIES MOVIES

USE : empty cardboard canister (potato chips and ice cream come in them) or make one by rolling stiff cardboard into a cylinder.

MAKE, borrow or buy a lazy susan (about $2 at most hardware stores, in plastic.)

1. Cut slots about 3" up from bottom, every 2" all the way around, leaving about ½" between slots.

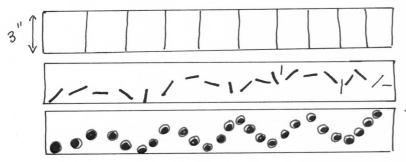

3"

Cut with a serrated kitchen knife or sharp scissors

2. Cut strips of paper to fit inside canister

3. Draw action sequence; stick spinning, ball bouncing, boy running, man going up-stairs, fish swimming, flower growing etc.
4. Place movie inside canister, picture side showing. Look through the slots —
5. Spin the Lazy Susan — see the action.

P.S. The movie needs to be well lit
   the drawing needs to be good + dark.
   the inside of canister can be painted black.

KITES · KITES · KITES ·

Kites brought electricity down to earth.
Kites took souls to heaven.
Kites were used for signals
   during the world wars.
Kites gave man an understanding
   of air currents
   balance
   wind changes
   gliding
   and the ratio of the surface
   area to weight.

Kites have always
delighted mankind
of all ages.

Someone flew 165 yards of silver mylar on a hoop frame, but you need a hill and lots of friends to gather it in.

I saw this fellow at the Great Boston Kite Festival flying a tiny tetrahedron.

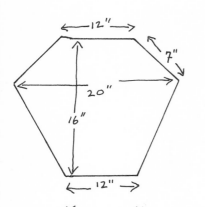

fantastic

PLASTIC BAG SLED KITE

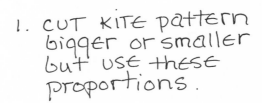

flies indoors and out !

1. CUT KITE pattern bigger or smaller but use these proportions.

   use plastic storage bag for greater strength (paper bag will do).

2. Tape 2 sticks from X to Y.

3. Attach bridle at A. and B. (Bridle should be twice the width of the kite).

4. make loop at center of bridle string C. and tie on Flying string.

5. Tape on 3 or 5 rag tails.

6. Find a wind or run fast!

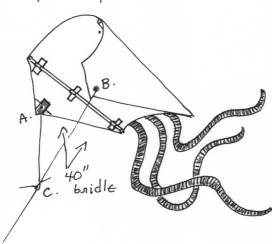

CARDBOARD RACING TURTLES

A good laugh is like sunshine in the house, my grandfather said.

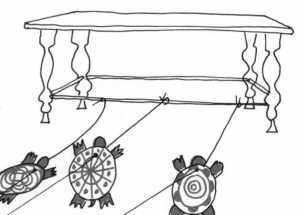

my mother introduced this game to us as children and I've never seen it played anywhere. Yet it is so simple and such fun especially when grown-ups join in.

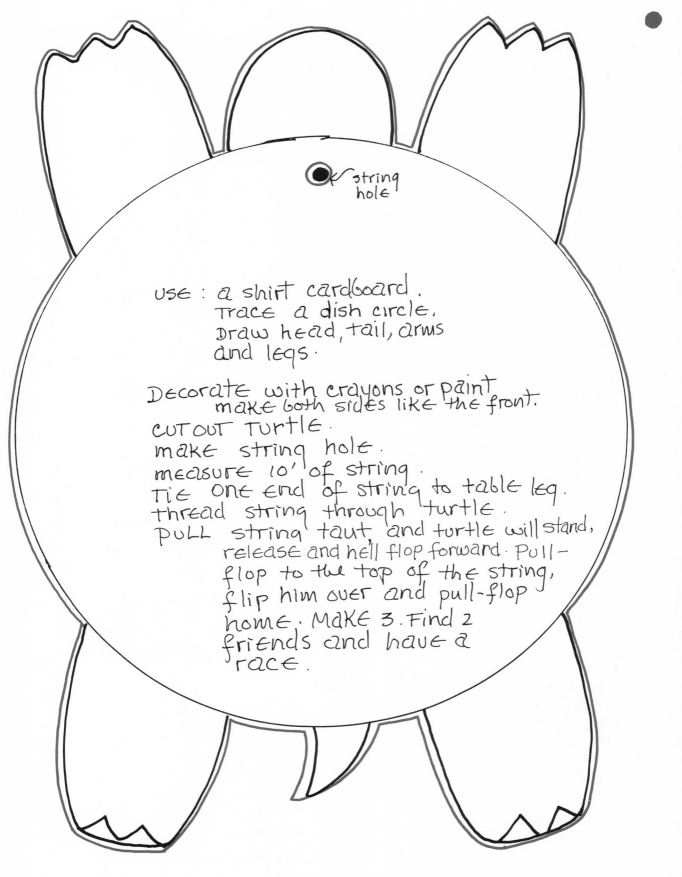

string hole

USE: a shirt cardboard.
Trace a dish circle.
Draw head, tail, arms
and legs.

Decorate with crayons or paint
make both sides like the front.
CUTOUT TURTLE.
make string hole.
measure 10' of string.
Tie one end of string to table leg.
thread string through turtle.
PULL string taut, and turtle will stand,
release and he'll flop forward. Pull-
flop to the top of the string,
flip him over and pull-flop
home. Make 3. Find 2
friends and have a
race.

TWISTING

Lots of people don't stop and think about how things are made and why.

I wouldn't devote a page to twisting if I hadn't witnessed hundreds of times, the excitement of school children who had just learned to make twist belts.

It is too simple to believe yet it is a true discovery. All you need is a piece of string.

For a belt use :
5 or more strands of yarn (different colors)
4 times your waist measure.

1. Attach one end of the yarns to hook, knob or something stable.

2. Twist the other ends keeping tension between the stable end and the twisting end.

3. When twist is good and tight, hold the twisted strings taut with one hand.

4. Find and pinch the center with the other hand.

5. Keeping everything taut, bend A. to B.

6. Tie A. & B. together

7. Let go of the center and the yarns or strings will spin together in a double reverse twist that will stay put.

P.S. Twisted string has double strength !

ROPE WINDING

Make an "automatic" block & coat hanger Model:

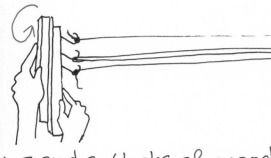

(The more strands the fatter the rope. Use colored yarns and wear it as a belt.)

1. Sand 2 blocks of wood approx. 2" x 12" x 1" pine.

2. Clamp both pieces of wood together and drill 3 holes 1½" apart starting 1" from the end.

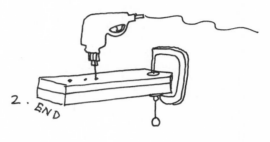

3. Cut 3 equal sections of coat hanger wire approx. 5¼" long.

4. Bend 1" foot in each wire carefully and exact.

5. Poke wires through 1st block, until foot rests flat on block.

6. Bend wire back against underside ⌐ zig zag

7. Thread 2nd block onto wires

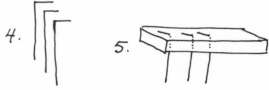

8. Bend wires backward about 30° angle

9. Use pliers to form hooks.

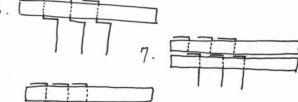

10. Action:
    Hold one block in each hand and rotate.

11. Tie on strings or yarns as shown above, from hook a. to doorknob back to hook b. to doorknob back to hook c. Tie and cut.

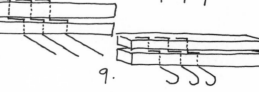

12. Rotate until twisted tight. Remove string from hooks. Tie ends together. Keeping tension, remove strings from doorknob and let go. All strands will spin together and stay put.

OVER & UNDER WEAVING

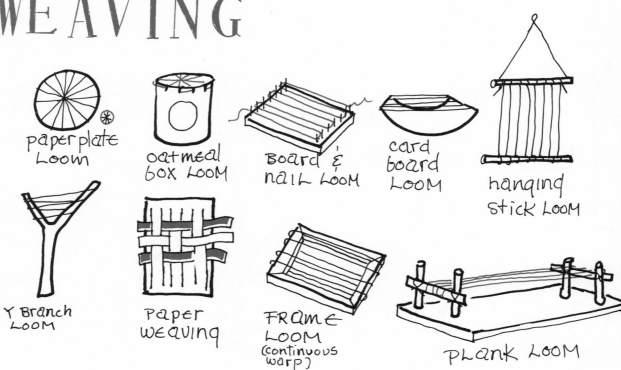

paper plate Loom

oatmeal box Loom

Board & nail Loom

card board Loom

hanging stick Loom

Y Branch Loom

paper weaving

FRAME LOOM (continuous warp)

PLANK LOOM

Man, Birds and Insects WEAVE !

Probably one of the first wonders!, enabling man to make a FABRIC for shelter, covering for his tender flesh, hammocks to hang from trees and nets and baskets to catch and carry and KEEP things in.

You can WEAVE sticks grasses, LEAVES, paper strings, yarns, and fingers.

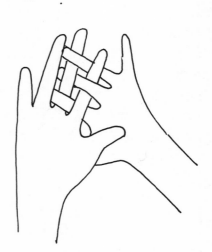

(note ✱ all round Loom weaving must have an odd number of strings.)

90

THE HEDDLE

Boredom has always forced man to find new and better ways.

Man said: HO-HUM HOW CAN I SPEED THIS UP? and with a little ingenious logic he invented THE **HEDDLE**

The HEDDLE, by opening the shed, made it possible to go over the over strings or under the under strings all at the same time. (Try it with a stick). The Problem was how to open both sheds alternating up and down. The solution was: 2 HEDDLE Bars with loops.

opening the shed

HEDDLE

2 HEDDLE BARS WITH LOOPS

ALL LOOMS can be fitted with HEDDLES, and to share man's wonderful discovery — you must try the HOLE & SLOT POPSICLE STICK LOOM and THE PEG & BOARD INKLE LOOM or the no-cost grocery BOX and stick INKLE model. page 93, 94

PLASTIC DRINKING STRAW BELT LOOM

Probably the first straw loom was made of straw or thin hollow Bamboo sticks (even stiff macaroni will do) but we have plastic drinking straws free at any ice cream parlor.

<u>USE</u> 4 or 5 straws. for small hands measure 5 strings twice your waist size. Thread or suck strings up each straw

Tape the end of each string to each straw, so it won't pull down and out. Tie a knot at the bottom to make a tassel. (A.)

(B.)

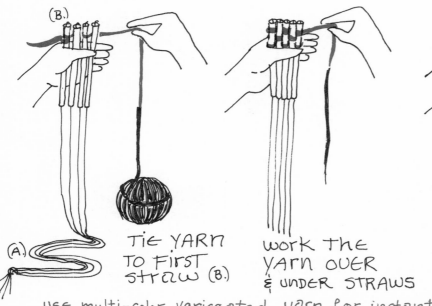

TIE YARN TO FIRST STRAW (B.)

work the YARN OVER & UNDER STRAWS

as the weaving fills the straws, push weaving down onto the strings, <u>only</u> an inch at a time as you need space. If weaving gets tight pull the straws up instead of pushing the weaving down. At the end, cut off straws and tie a tassel.

use multi-color variegated yarn for instant patterns instead of tying on different colors.

POPSICLE STICK HEDDLE LOOM

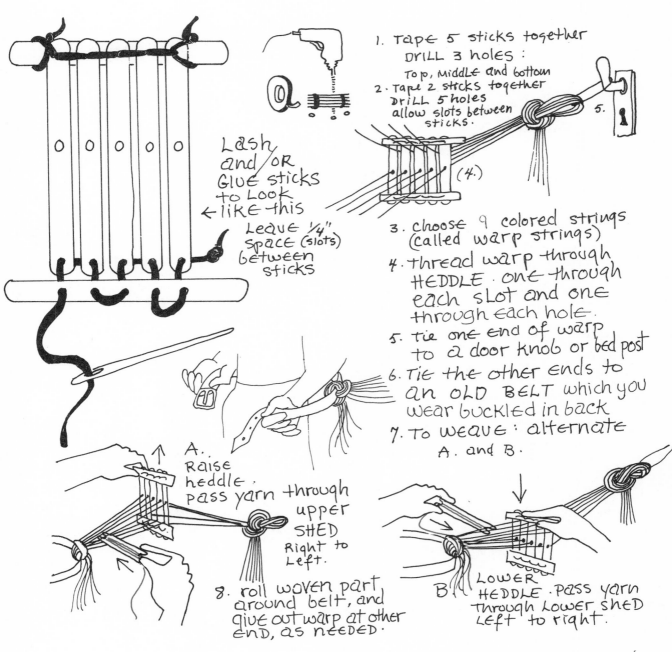

1. Tape 5 sticks together DRILL 3 holes:
   Top, Middle and Bottom
2. Tape 2 sticks together DRILL 5 holes allow slots between sticks.

Lash and/or GLUE sticks to LOOK ←like this

Leave 1/4" space (slots) between sticks

3. choose 9 colored strings (called warp strings)
4. thread warp through HEDDLE. one through each slot and one through each hole.
5. tie one end of warp to a door knob or bed post
6. Tie the other ends to an OLD BELT which you wear buckled in back
7. To WEAVE: alternate A. and B.

A. Raise heddle. pass yarn through upper SHED Right to Left.

8. roll woven part around belt, and give out warp at other end, as needed.

B. LOWER HEDDLE. pass yarn through LOWER SHED LEFT to right.

trust me — it will work, even though the words sound complicated.

BOX & STICK INKLE LOOM

In order to make heddle Looms available to hundreds of children in public schools without an art budget, we adapted the common corrugated packing box as shown here.

EVERY child could make and own an Inkle Loom at no cost.

YOU NEED ½ an hour
a grocery box approx. 12"x12"x18"
5 sticks or dowels 2" wider than box.

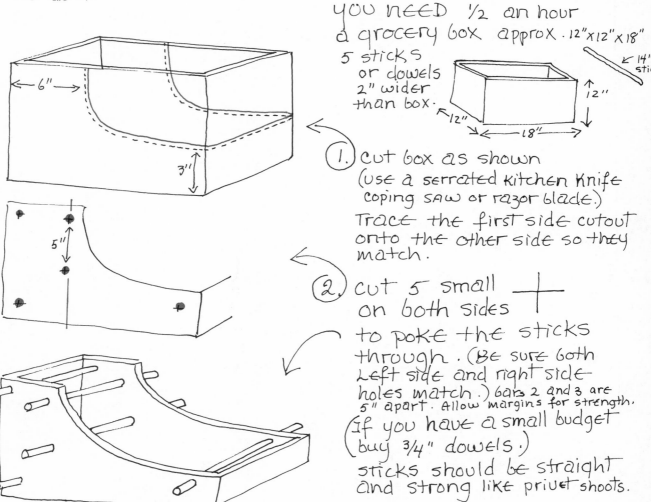

1. cut box as shown (use a serrated kitchen knife coping saw or razor blade.) Trace the first side cutout onto the other side so they match.

2. cut 5 small + on both sides to poke the sticks through. (Be sure both left side and right side holes match.) bars 2 and 3 are 5" apart. Allow margins for strength. (If you have a small budget buy ¾" dowels.) sticks should be straight and strong like privet shoots.

please note: with a little adjustment you can adapt boxes of many other dimensions.

Tying heddle Loops   for belt or headband

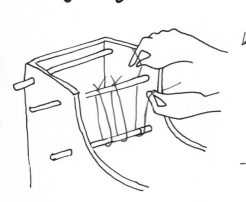

1. Tie 3 Loops as shown around bars 2 and 3 then slip the bars out so you can remove Loops.

2. Double each loop and slip them over bar 2 (the heddle bar)

Warping your Loom

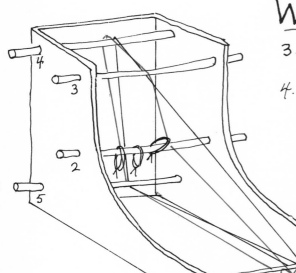

3. Cut 6 or more strings about 48" long.

4. Follow Route A and route B alternating each string. All the A strings go from bar 1 to bar 4, under bar 5, under bar 1 and tie in a bow. All the B strings go from bar 1, through double heddle loop on bar 2, over bars 3 and 4, under bars 5 and 1, and tie in a bow.

Route A

Route B

To WEAVE
raise and lower sheds with finger

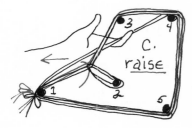

C. raise

D. Lower

C. Raise strings under peg 3 and pass weaving yarn through shed right to Left.

D. Lower strings under peg 3 and pass yarn through shed left to right.

Continue alternating C and D until woven part is 3" or 4". Slide woven part backwards toward peg 5. When woven part reaches peg 3, untie warp bows. Remove weaving from Loom. Tie a tassel at both ends and wear it!

WEAVING IN MATH CLASS

Becky Corwin at the children's MUSEUM RESOURCE CENTER says: "why not—

warp your loom and assign a numeral to each string. Then— as you mutter the over–under song as you weave back and forth think about odds and evens."

1 2 3 4 5 6 7 8

skip counting on 9 strings:

"now go on to skip-counting: pick up every third string start with #3 then pick up the 6th string, then the 9th going left to right"

(an easy way to learn the TIMES tables .....)

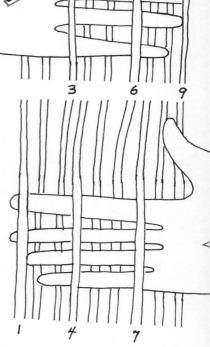

3 6 9

on the next row pick up every third string: 7, 4 and 1 going from right to left. see what pattern it makes...

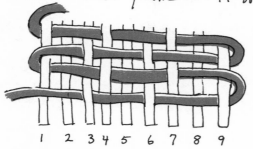

1 2 3 4 5 6 7 8 9

1 4 7

✳︎ try _all_ kinds of combinations, it's hand-logic-math."

96

square number weaving, algebra
and the <u>binomial theorem</u>: in two dimensions.

$$(red + black)^2 = red^2 + 2\,red/black + black^2$$
$$\underline{or}\ (a + b)^2 = a^2 + 2\,ab + b^2$$

1. warp 8 red and 4 black strings.
    (or multiples, like 32 red and 16 black)

2. weave 8 red rows
    and then 4 black rows

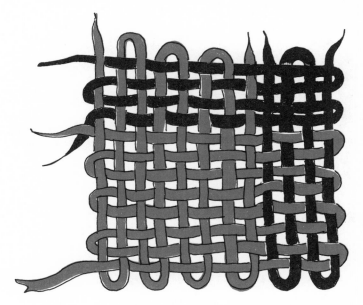

3. what do you see?
   what did you prove!

   ✓ right: $(a+b)^2 = a^2 + 2\,ab + b^2$

THE BINOMIAL THEOREM

WEED WEAVING

on natural structures

An autumn trip to the beach and the marsh provides beautiful raw materials for nature weavings on natural structures.

Look for driftwood, Queen Anne's Lace, wheats and long stalks, all kinds of grasses and dry weeds, milkweed, cattails vetch and vines, flotsam and kelp, fibers and feathers, corn husks, leaves, bark, bamboo and reeds

Japan Nissan
Island Bow
Loom

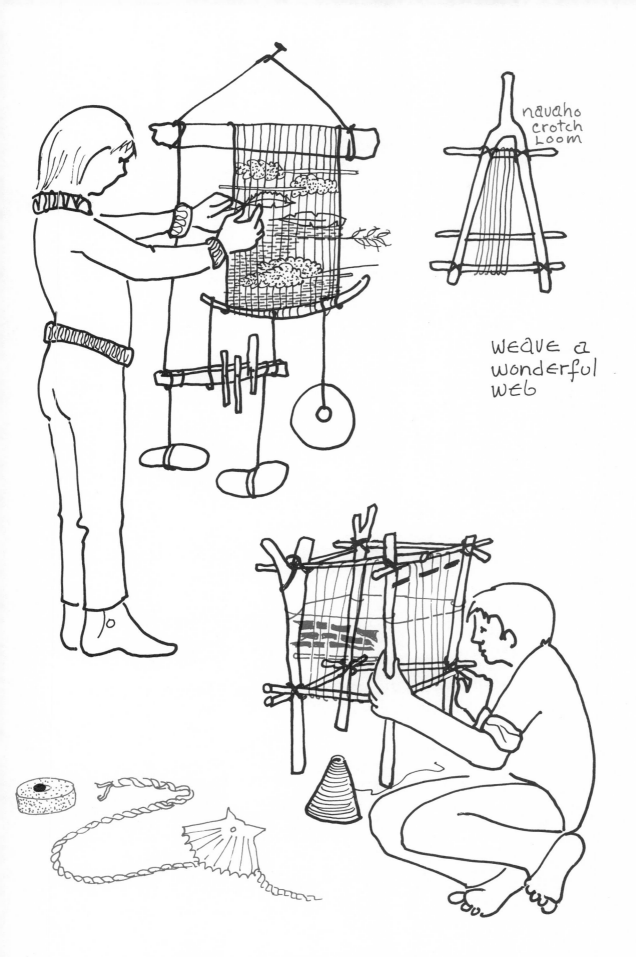

navaho
crotch
Loom

WEAVE a
wonderful
WEb

MACRAMÉ SAILORS LACE

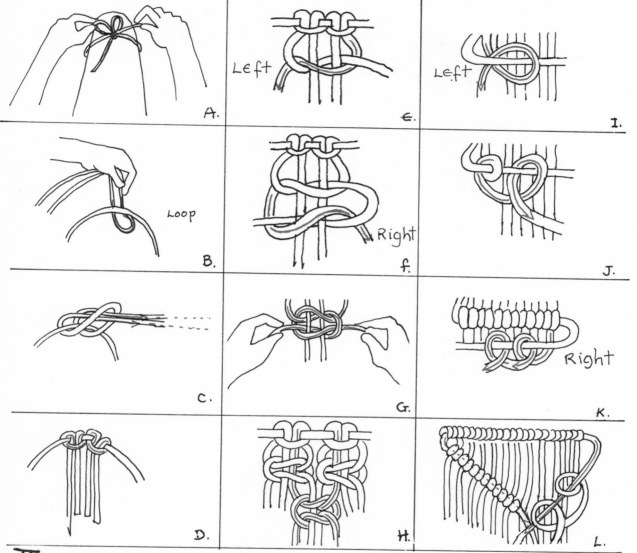

A.

Left — E.

Left — I.

Loop — B.

Right — F.

J.

C.

G.

Right — K.

D.

H.

L.

The knee harness is very comfortable for small work.

A. Tie holding cord around your knee
B. Hitch strings to cord in multiples of 4.
C. Beginners start with 2 strings 24" long. Hitch the loop middle to holding cord.
D. Make 4 or more strings ready 12" long.

The Square Knot has a left and a right part tied around the 2 center strings.

E. Right over left
F. Left over right
G. Pull square knot into shape.
H. Shows how you join strings on second row.

The half hitch must be double to hold tight.

A row of half hitches can be set horizontally or diagonally.

I. The left outside string acts as cross bar.
J. Each string hitches around cross bar twice.
K. To hitch from the right side: reverse method.
L. Hitching on a diagonal.

4 String Easy Macramé belt

Use heavy mason's twine or venetian blind cord.
1. Measure 4 strings 48" long or 60" if you're big.
2. Tie a tassel knot to hold the 4 strings together.
3. Hold tassel between toes or tie it to a chair or knee.
4. Hold the 2 middle strings in your teeth or belt.
5. Tie square knots as shown in fig. E.F.G.
6. About half way (15") switch strings. continue knotting with long strings on the outside, short ones in your teeth or belt.

If 48" of string is too hard to handle, tie it in a butterfly:

and let them out as you need more string.

The Spiral
is made by tying only half a square knot: the Left side all the way down or the right side fig. E. or f. (Let it turn over as you go) switch to short strings midway.

MACRAMÉ NECKLACE SAMPLER

USE thin mason's twine
1. Cut 9 strings 30" long
2. Tie one string around your knee
   slide bow knot to back of leg
3. Hitch the other 8 strings onto
   the knee string as in fig. D.
4. Tie 3 rows of square knots across
   (16 strings make 4 square knots.)
5. Using left outside string tie 2
   rows of half hitches (left and right)
6. Spiral on each 4 strings
   make 4 spirals about 1" long.

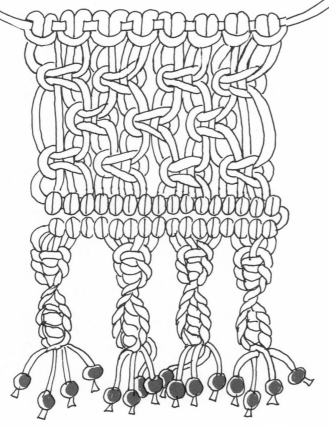

If you have beads
that fit your string
thread them on
the neck string and
at the end of spirals.

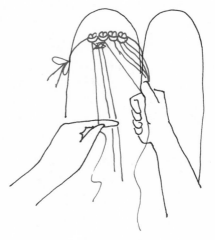

102

LOVE POUCH

for little macramé experts.

use medium fine linen or cotton crochet twine

1. Cut one string 90" long and tie it around knee
2. Cut 27 strings 32" long and hitch them on.
3. Cut one string 60" long and hitch it onto knee string at far left so half of it is the same length as the others and the rest gives you a long string for hitching crossbars.
4. Now you have 56 strings all 16" long but crossbar
5. make 2 rows of double half hitches. from left to right and back again.
6. make 3 rows of square knots.
7. make 2 rows of double half hitches.
8. make 13 rows of square knots.
9. make 2 rows of double half hitches
10. make 3 rows of square knots
11. untie holding cord from knee and fold macramé in half. Find center of holding string and pull gently until you have equal parts on both sides of pouch. Tie onto knee.
12. Using the long crossbar string, make 2 rows of double half hitches on every other string — thus closing the bottom.
13. Sew up open side of pouch.
14. **neck string**: Tie knots on holding strings: one left one right. all the way up on each side. Then tie them all together.

103

BO'SUN'S MACRAMÉ KEEL LOOM

remembered by Edward Montgomery.

my kids macramé off the back of a chair holding the stable strings in their teeth or tucked in their belt. I macramé small things off my knee. But Edward says his Bo'sun's mate used the keel loom and made me this little model. Try it.

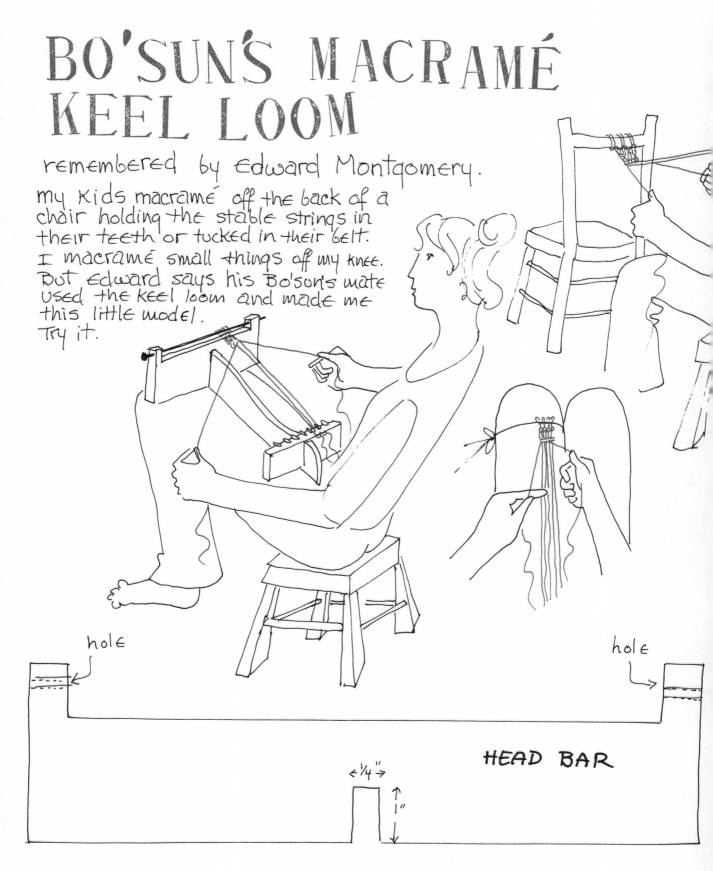

hole

hole

←¼"→

HEAD BAR

1"

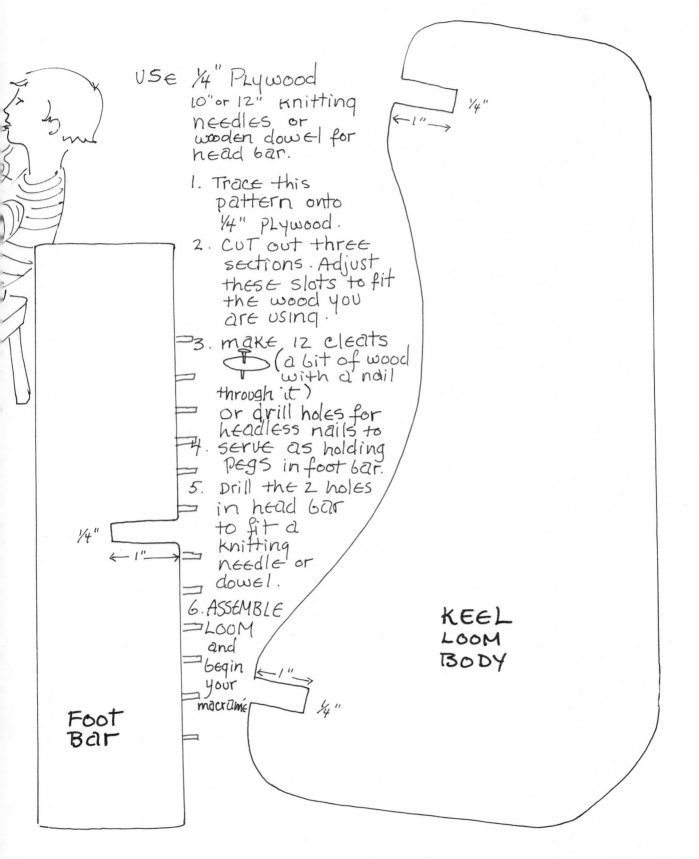

USE ¼" PLYWOOD
10" or 12" knitting
needles or
wooden dowel for
head bar.

1. Trace this
   pattern onto
   ¼" plywood.

2. CUT out three
   sections. Adjust
   these slots to fit
   the wood you
   are using.

3. make 12 cleats
   (a bit of wood
   with a nail
   through it)
   or drill holes for
   headless nails to

4. serve as holding
   pegs in foot bar.

5. Drill the 2 holes
   in head bar
   to fit a
   knitting
   needle or
   dowel.

6. ASSEMBLE
   LOOM
   and
   begin
   your
   macramé

¼"
← 1" →

Foot
Bar

← 1" →
¼"

KEEL
LOOM
BODY

← 1" →
¼"

105

RYA TUFTING

or oriental knotting.

The language of knotting
is : to __PUT__ a knot (to tie)
to __spill__ a knot (undo)

The Turkish ghiordes knot

USE: a coarse woven fabric
like monks cloth , burlap
or rug backing. Rug needle
and yarns.
1. Start bottom left corner
(if you are right-handed).
2. Put one knot, as shown
on every 2 warp strings
3. Continue left to
right across
bottom row.
4. Cut extending
tuft about 1"
or as you wish.
(cut as you go or
all at the end of each row.)

warp

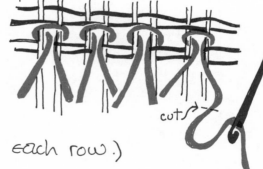

cut

You can follow a color pattern
and work section by section.
You can have high or low pile.
You can make an oriental rug
or a shaggy vest.

That's all there is to it: one knot again and again.

TUFTED SHAGGY VEST

cut: vest pattern out of monks cloth or burlap

1. measure a jacket or sweater that fits you as a guide
2. cut front & back of vest together
3. sew sides together
4. cut front piece open and cut throat-chest opening as desired.
5. using the Rya tufting method, knot shaggy yarn into the warp threads of your vest.

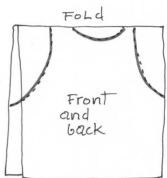

FOLD

Front and back

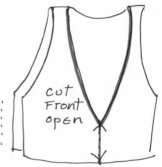

cut front open

BODY COVERING

When I was a student living in Paris, I learned a lot about the logic of simple economical patterns for body covering.

Necessity is the mother of improvisation and the French are thrifty and clever.

While bicycling through the chateau country Monique invited me to visit her home in the Loire valley. We had picked up fabrics in the marketplace and wanted to make skirts. "Patterns are for people who don't understand body logic." she explained.

Monique's Body-logic Straight Skirt

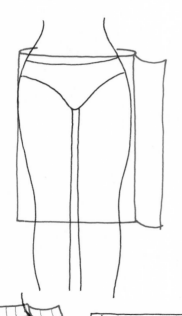

1. Since your hips are the widest part of you, wrap your fabric around your hips like a straight tube to determine the width of your skirt. Sew seams together. except for 5" at top for zipper. Left side.

2. All hips curve so cut a slow 8" 2" curve at both sides. sew curve seam.

3. measure your waist. measure your hips. Adjust the difference by making 2 darts in front and 2 darts in back. sew. & press.

4. sew zipper in by hand. it's easier.

5. waist band : sew grosgrain ribbon to front side of skirt waist. ribbon back-

6. then fold ward and inside. stitch to

FIN.

BODY LOGIC CLOTHES

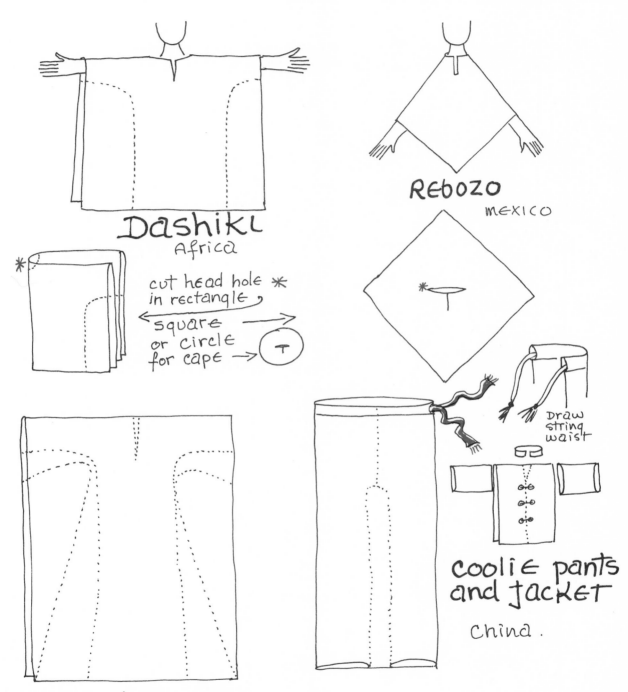

Dashiki Africa

cut head hole * in rectangle,

← square →
or circle
for cape →

Rebozo MEXICO

Draw string waist

Coolie pants and Jacket
China.

Caftan & Burnoose
India & Asia.

QUICK CLOTHES ♀ ♂
Basic caftan-coat-dress-robe-shirt.

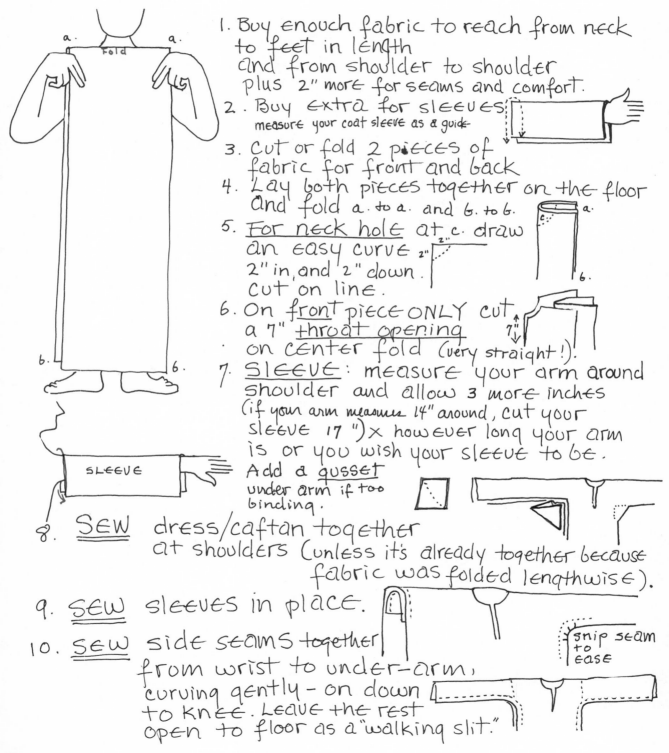

1. Buy enough fabric to reach from neck to feet in length and from shoulder to shoulder plus 2" more for seams and comfort.

2. Buy extra for sleeves; measure your coat sleeve as a guide

3. Cut or fold 2 pieces of fabric for front and back

4. Lay both pieces together on the floor and fold a. to a. and b. to b.

5. For neck hole at c. draw an easy curve 2" in, and 2" down. Cut on line.

6. On front piece ONLY cut a 7" throat opening on center fold (very straight!).

7. SLEEVE: measure your arm around shoulder and allow 3 more inches (if your arm measures 14" around, cut your sleeve 17")x however long your arm is or you wish your sleeve to be. Add a gusset under arm if too binding.

8. SEW dress/caftan together at shoulders (unless it's already together because fabric was folded lengthwise).

9. SEW sleeves in place.

10. SEW side seams together from wrist to under-arm, curving gently - on down to knee. Leave the rest open to floor as a "walking slit."

snip seam to ease

11. HEM SLEEVES
    walking slit and
    bottom edges
    neck and throat.

A. EASIEST WAY: Fray edges

B. EASY WAY: Buy bias
   binding of a complementary
   color and sew it onto
   all the raw edges.
   Either letting it show
   like piping or turning it
   all under as an inner
   facing.

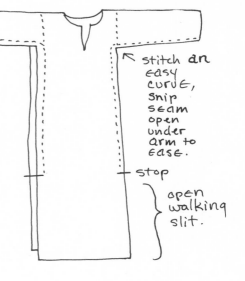

← stitch an
easy
curve,
snip
seam
open
under
arm to
ease.

— stop

} open walking slit.

Variations and adaptations:

This basic model can be:

wider
like a
night
shirt
cut from
cotton
flannel

sleeveless
and slinky
cut out of
Jersey or
Banlon.

A-Shaped
cut from
wider cloth

A winter
coat, open
up the front
with a fur
collar sewn
on.

A zipper
Jacket
with a
knitted
collar

a beach
or bath
robe.
Belted

A basic
Dress
to Batik
or Tie-dye

A ski shirt
for your
Lover

A
Bunting
for your
baby

what more can you possibly
need?...........

TIE - DYE

an ancient art

When early man sat on his first Berry
he discovered dye.
Tying came much later –
but when dying and tying got together
man saw the knot resist the dye.

USE: starch-free cloth: cotton T-shirts,
bedsheeting, silk, muslin, etc.

Many ways to Tie and Dye:
with thread or rubber bands, and
natural or commercial dyes.

twist

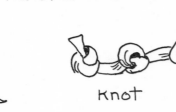

knot

tie

puff

pleat

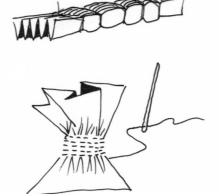

stitch

roll

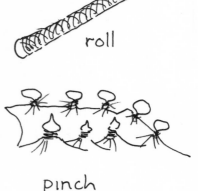

pinch

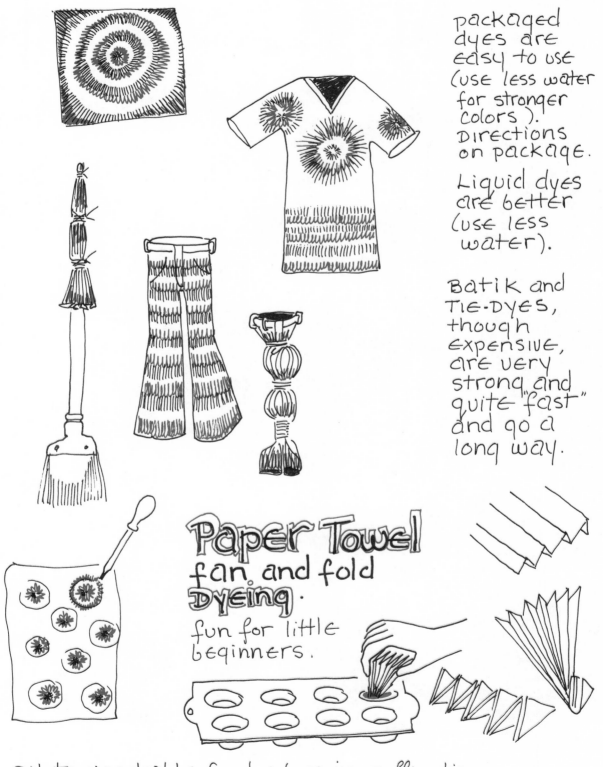

packaged
dyes are
easy to use
(use less water
for stronger
colors).
Directions
on package.

Liquid dyes
are better
(use less
water).

Batik and
TIE-DYES,
though
expensive,
are very
strong and
quite "fast"
and go a
long way.

Paper Towel
fan and fold
~~Dyeing~~.
fun for little
beginners.

Dilute vegetable food colors in muffin tin
Fold paper towels and dip, unfold and dry.
Try eye dropper drops on wet paper towels.

QUICK BATIK wax resist

can be done on paper or cloth with wax crayons
melted candle stubs, paraffin or bees wax

Paper method crayon resist:

1. Draw a picture or design
   with crayons. press hard
   and cover all the paper.
2. Now scrumple it up.
3. now smooth it out
   and paint over it with
   ebony stain, ink or thin
   poster black. The
   cracking gives it
   a nice antique look.

Cloth and hot wax resist

1. Paint designs on almost any white or light-
   colored fabric. Bed sheets torn small are perfect.

a word of **CAUTION**: Heating wax can
be **VERY DANGEROUS. Use a double
boiler. Dont let it boil or smoke or
leave it unwatched.**

you need: cheap brushes,
a box of paraffin. Double boiler
Hot plate. Pot holder. Iron.
old coffee can. DYES, SALT
Lots of news paper and pans.

1. Draw on cloth with hot wax
   (it should penetrate the cloth and
   look transparent in order to
   resist the dye later on).
2. Paint on colored dyes. use
   5 and 10 cold water dyes and
   add a big spoon of salt to each
   color.
3. Iron cloth between newspapers.
   to remove wax and dry it quickly.

BATIK is an ancient
and noble ART
with many refinements
but you can
get a taste
of it

using This
QUICK Method
PLEASE
Be careful

LOVE YOU

FOOT GLOVES

Use a piece of leather 1 foot wide by however long your foot is.

1. Make a paper pattern. Trace your foot on a brown paper bag.
2. Cut a shape sort of like this around your foot tracing. 12" wide.
3. Put your foot in place on pattern and wrap flaps over instep
4. Draw a line behind where toes bend. Cut toe line.
5. Draw line from inside of heel (arch A.) to top of foot, and around to outside of heel.
6. Cut on these lines.
7. Decide where the flaps should join and make a slash
8. Make a holding knob on the other flap with neck same size as slash width.
9. Cut 2 of your pattern from leather, one side up for left foot, other side up for right foot.

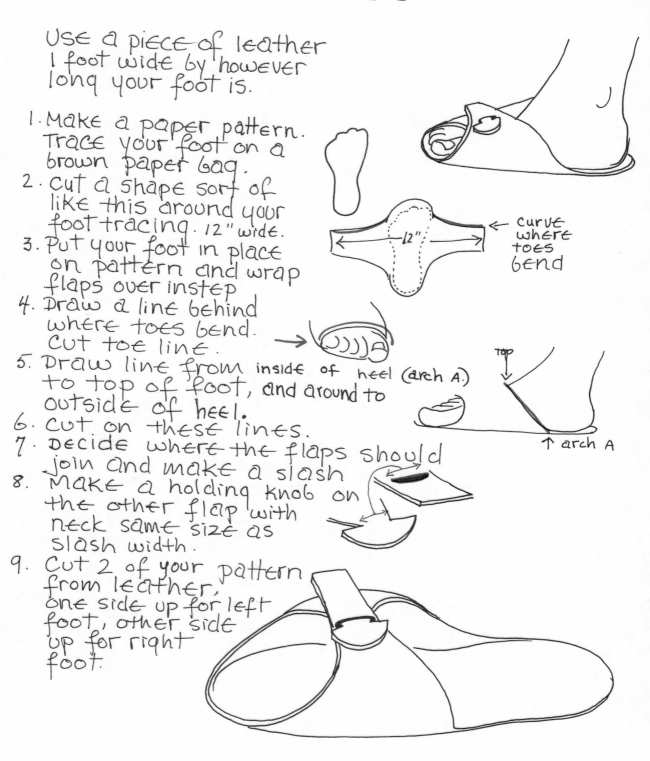

← curve where toes bend

12"

top ↓

↑ arch A

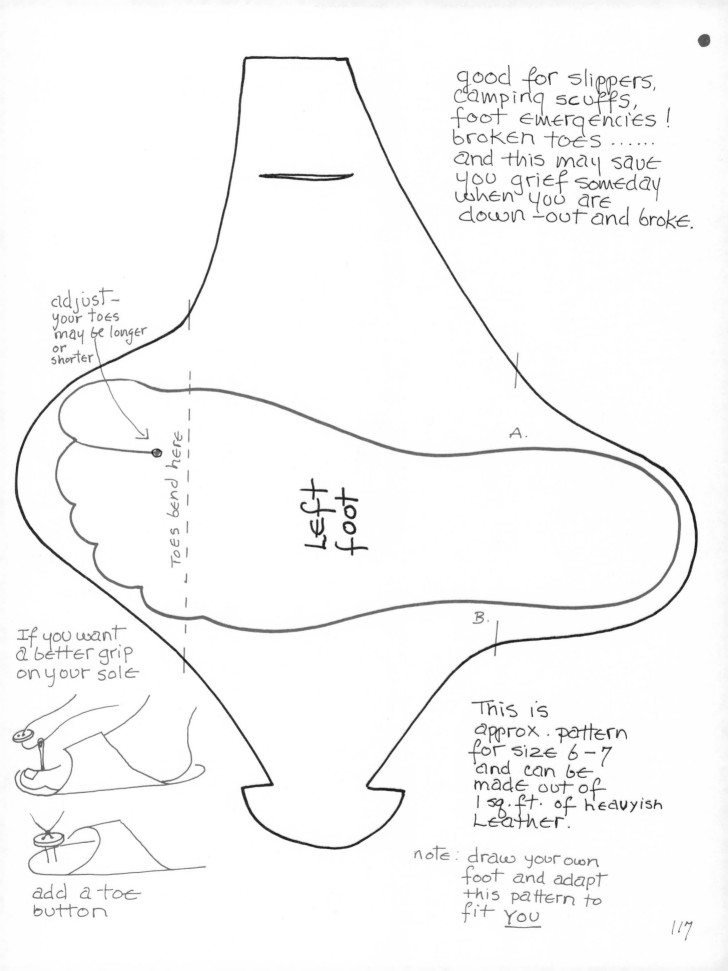

good for slippers,
camping scuffs,
foot emergencies!
broken toes ......
and this may save
you grief someday
when you are
down -out and broke.

adjust-
your toes
may be longer
or
shorter

Toes bend here

Left foot

A.

B.

If you want
a better grip
on your sole

add a toe
button

This is
approx. pattern
for size 6 – 7
and can be
made out of
1 sq. ft. of heavyish
Leather.

note: draw your own
foot and adapt
this pattern to
fit YOU

117

STOCKING MASKS

from nylon stockings
and wire coat
hangers.

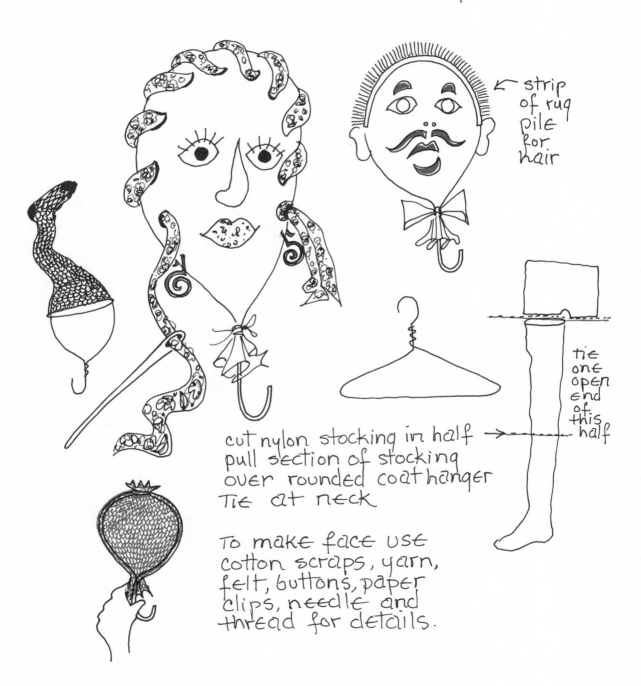

strip
of rug
pile
for
hair

cut nylon stocking in half →
pull section of stocking
over rounded coat hanger
Tie at neck

tie
one
open
end
of
this
half

To make face use
cotton scraps, yarn,
felt, buttons, paper
clips, needle and
thread for details.

Many secrets can be told
behind a mask.
Shyness is hidden.

If you make a bold boy mask
you can tell your teacher you love her
or that her classes are boring.

If you make a wise and thoughtful mask
you can explain things —
even things you didn't think you understood.

If you make a new-person mask
you can be someone new
the person you'd like to be.

Little and big people as well,
wish to change:
from rough to gentle
from stupid to wise
from scared to brave
from shy to bold
from indifferent to caring

You can practice being new, behind a mask,
until it becomes the real you.
or the better you.

my son said
"I am only bad
if you say I am bad..."
and "I am funny
when I tickle inside."

BOX COSTUMES

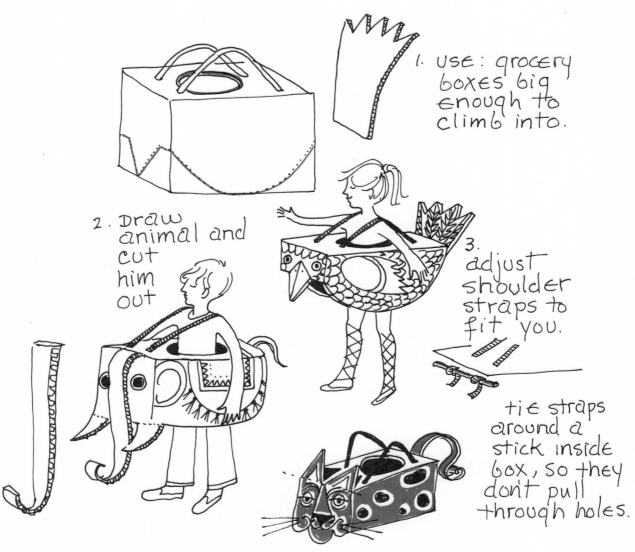

1. use: grocery boxes big enough to climb into.

2. Draw animal and cut him out

3. adjust shoulder straps to fit you.

tie straps around a stick inside box, so they don't pull through holes.

good for plays, parades and Halloween.

BOX SCULPTURE

from milk cartons and shoe boxes, egg crates and paper towel tubes.

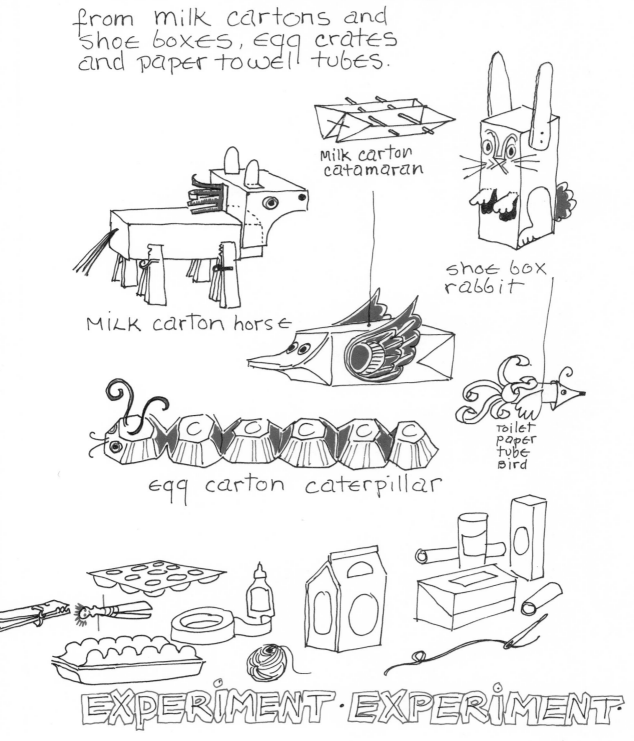

milk carton catamaran

shoe box rabbit

MILK carton horse

egg carton caterpillar

toilet paper tube Bird

EXPERIMENT · EXPERIMENT·

ODD SOCK PUPPETS

Make a family of puppets.
LIBERATE THE ODD SOCK
characters.
Decorate with
Buttons. Beads
Felt scraps
Rug scraps
Fringes. Yarn
rick rack

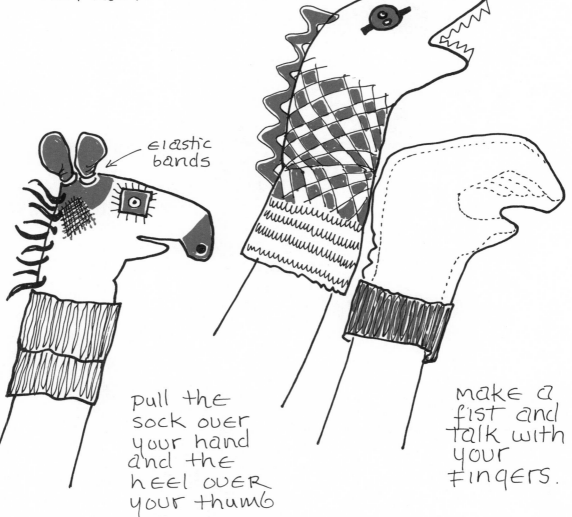

elastic
bands

Pull the
sock over
your hand
and the
heel over
your thumb

make a
fist and
talk with
your
fingers.

ODD GLOVE FINGER PUPPETS

cut off fingers
of glove.

decorate
sew
glue
paste

elastic
band

MOUTH
EYES
NOSE
HAIR
BEAK
WHISKERS

123

UNUSUAL
BUBBLES

fill the dish pan with
warm water and a good
splash of detergent

small bubble pipes can
be made out of wire

and juice cans with
a hole at the other end
or beer cans with bottom
out

Tape
3 cans
together

Blow a dome
on a cookie tray

But best of all and biggest o o o o o
are bubbles made with glycerine & soap
on a plastic straw & string frame.
A wonderful discovery enlarged
at The Boston Children's Museum
to delight little & big Bubble lovers.

see: <u>Soap Bubbles and the forces which Mould Them</u> by c. v. Boys
Doubleday Anchor Books from EDC's science study series.

have an exciting hilarious bubble launching party!

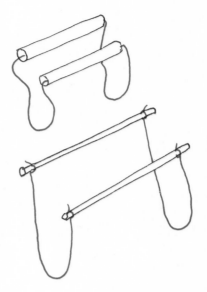

1. thread 1 yard of string through plastic drinking straws

   or

   Tie string to 2 sticks or thin dowels.

2. Drop this contraption in your pan of detergent to which you can add a dollop of Glycerine *

   * Glycerine gives the soap film more elasticity and iridescence.
   you can buy a jar at the drug store.

3. gather a film across the strings pull the straws apart to stretch the film open.
4. Pull upwards filling the film with air gently
5. Relax the contraption and snap the bubble free of the frame -FANTASTIC!

AVOCADO PEAR TREE

TOP ↑ ↓ base

Florida   california

  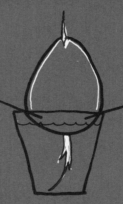 

spear with
3 tooth picks.
set in water

root

stem
and
roots

alas...
snip off
first Leafing

The most amazing
Avocado Pit tree
I ever saw growing
indoors was in the
stairwell of The Addison
gallery in Andover, MASS.
It was 2 stories high
and 21 years old.

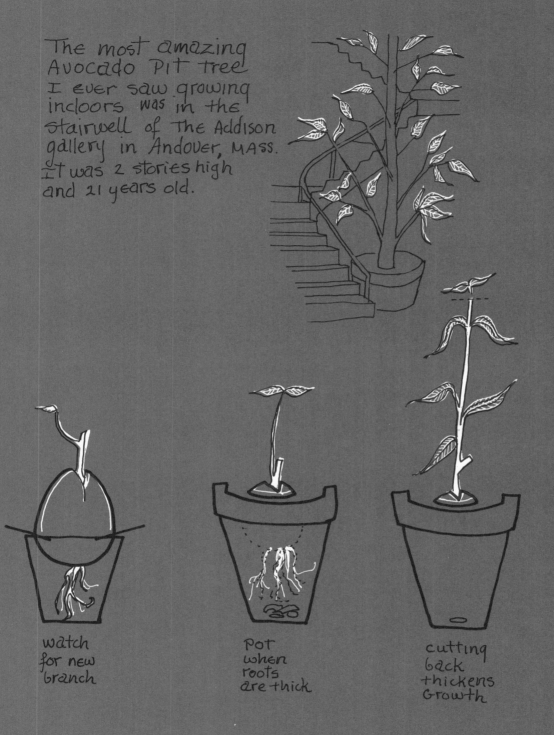

watch
for new
branch

pot
when
roots
are thick

cutting
back
thickens
Growth

There is a charming little Avocado Pit Growers
indoor How-to-book by H. Perper published
by Walker & Co if you are having trouble
with your green thumb.

CASTING PLASTER

plaster of Paris is temperamental.
It sets quickly.
It dries fast, but
it stays soggy
if the air is damp
or if the proportions are wrong.
It scratches easily
it breaks easily if dropped,
but it is easy to use:
good for building up sculpture
good for quick casting
good for plaster scrimshaw
pendants and rubbings,
and plaster blocks are good
for carving.

The hand plaque.
no matter how over worked the idea - it's pretty sweet
to have that little hand printed in plaster. Pour plaster of
Paris in small greased pie dish. Press hand into plaster mix
hold it just a moment or two until plaster sets.

SAND CASTING
with plaster of Paris (sunny dry days only)

If you can do this on the beach
the sea will wash away the mess.
An outdoor sand pile is good too
but a shoe box full of sand will do.

you will need a stick
         plastic bowl
         bucket of water
         5 lbs. plaster of Paris

1. Smooth surface in the <u>wet</u> sand
   with a shingle or your hand.

2. Draw your picture with a stick

3. decorate with fork or spoon
   marks, shell imprints, colored glass
   or beach pebbles

4. <u>MIX PLASTER</u>:
   enough to fill the area.
   pour water in bowl
   pour plaster powder into water
   until mountain peak rises
   above water level.
   stir until smooth

5. pour mixture quickly on top of drawing
   about 1 ½" to 2" thick

6. stick a paper clip into the wet plaster
   to act as a hanger

7. Allow plaster to set
   about 10 min. or until no longer warm.

8. Lift plaster out of sand, rinse in the sea
   and hang it up at home.

PLASTER SCRIMSHAW

1. Stir one cup of plaster of Paris into 2/3 cup water
2. Mix until thick and smooth (use quickly, it hardens fast!)
3. Drop spoonfuls like cookies on wax paper
4. Allow 5 to 10 minutes to harden.
   but introduce wire hanger or make hole while soft. →

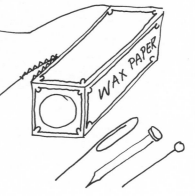

5. Use a nail or a pin to etch a design

You can scratch it. paint it. shellac it put a leather thong through it and wear it,

Or — you can make rubbings from it:
   put a sheet of paper on top of design and rub a crayon over it

Scrimshaw was the whalers' art of scratching on sharks' teeth and whale bone. Try soup bones!

PLASTER CARVING BLOCKS

1. pour mixed plaster of Paris into milk cartons or shoe boxes depending on how big a carving block you need!

2. when plaster is set (no longer warm) tear off box

3. You can carve block with kitchen tools or sculpture chisels

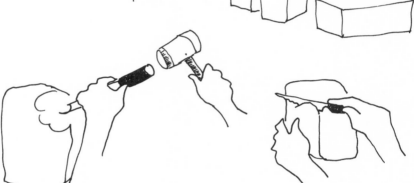

Master notes:
    Plaster block dipped in water makes carving easier.

    Salt in the plaster mix speeds thickening (that's why using the ocean is good).

    Oil or vaseline protects surfaces against plaster sticking to mold

    Vinegar retards drying.

    Coffee grounds or vermiculite added to plaster mix makes interesting easy-to-carve texture for sculpture.

    Wet plaster can also be used to build up form on an armature, then filed or sanded to perfection.

    Plastic bowls and buckets are best - rinse immediately. Caution: plaster clogs sink drain! dump it outside: drain water, separate plaster.

XYLOPHONE

USE: electrician's pipe: copper or steel.
(approx. 75¢ for 10 feet)
⑦₈" or ③₄" diameter
at hardware store
or lumber yard.

1. cut pipe lengths
with a hacksaw
or pipe cutter
using these
proportions

2. Lay pipes
across 2 strips
of wood padded
with rubber or
fabric or just
lay them across
two belts.

3. A pencil or
dowel

← Rubber band

makes
a good
hammer.

good xylophones are expensive but you shall have music!
(Ideas from EDC's Elementary Science Study Unit <u>Musical Instrument Recipe Book</u>.)

SWEET SOUNDS FROM FOUND OBJECTS

from the kitchen and the junk heap.

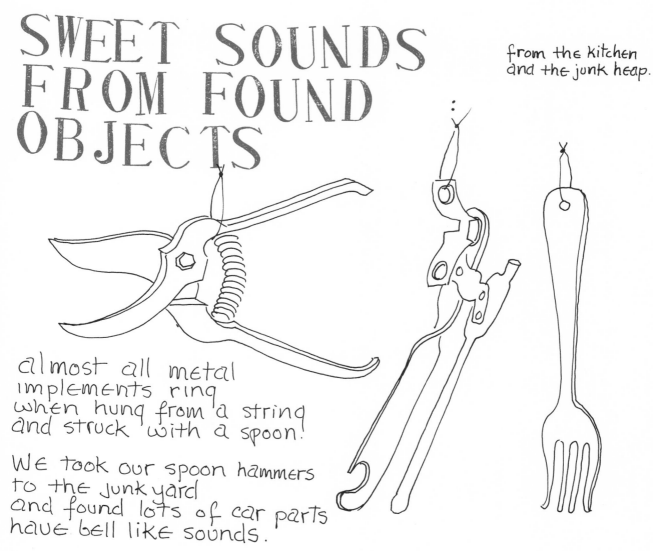

almost all metal implements ring when hung from a string and struck with a spoon!

We took our spoon hammers to the junk yard and found lots of car parts have bell like sounds.

You can collect a bunch of sounds. clean them with gasoline. Drill holes so you can hang them by strings. play them like timpani. Hub cap, body parts, gear wheel CACOPHONY!

don't just bang,

syncopate!

THUMB PIANO KAFFIR

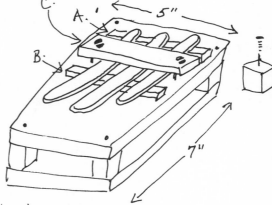

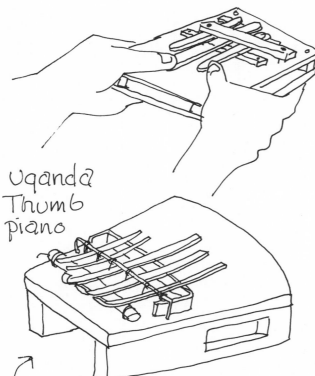

Uganda
Thumb
piano

This Uganda Thumb piano
is made out of Balsa wood
with steel tongues.
This, attached to a gourd
makes a fine sounding
box. note: The African
has no rule about scale
or order of note or length.
what sounds good, is good!

1. This simple adaptation is
   made out of a spruce board
   7"x 5" x ³/₁₆". Cut 2 for top
   and bottom. Plus cubes for legs.
2. Nail or glue 2 cross bars as
   shown A and B ½" apart
   (front bar should be a little higher
   than back strip 4"x ¼").
3. Lay 3 popsicle sticks across
   bars A and B so the extending
   parts over B are different
   lengths — thus making different sounds.
4. Screw third cross bar C (over
   center of popsicle sticks)
   to board, left and right. Tighten
   and play.

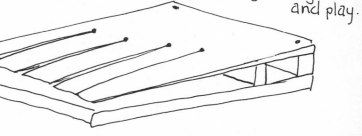

The Education Development
Center in Newton Mass., show people how to make Thumb
pianos out of cedar shingles: Thick end of shingle for
bottom, thin end for top part with splits different
widths and lengths for notes. See The E.S.S. Musical
Instrument Recipe Book · McGraw Hill · Webster Div. Manchester. Mo.

SHEPHERD'S PIPE

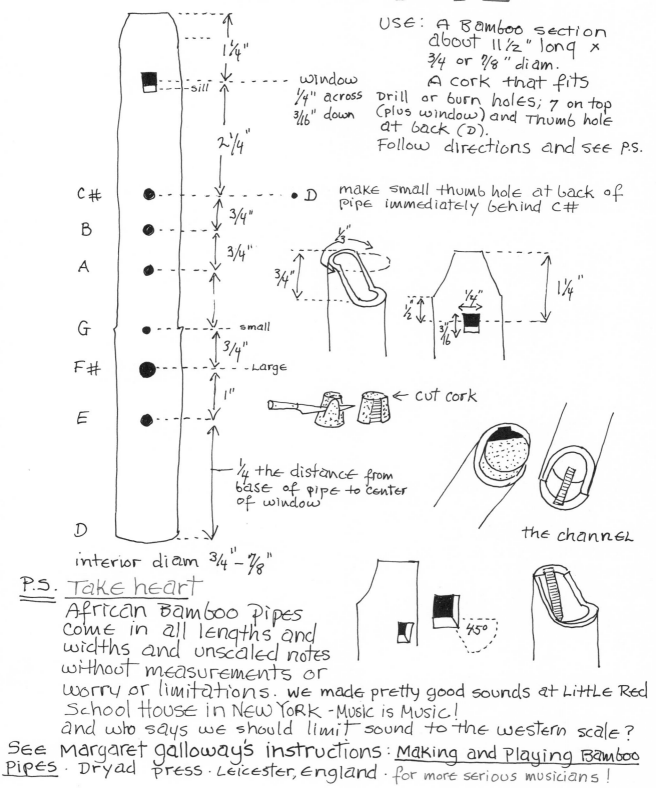

USE: A Bamboo section about 11½" long × ¾ or ⅞" diam.
A cork that fits

Drill or burn holes; 7 on top (plus window) and Thumb hole at back (D).
Follow directions and see P.S.

1¼"

─sill   window
          ¼" across
          3/16" down

2¼"

C#   • D   make small thumb hole at back of pipe immediately behind C#

B
        3/4"

A   3/4"

G   small

F#   Large
        3/4"

E   1"

¼ the distance from base of pipe to center of window

D

interior diam ¾" – ⅞"

← cut cork

the channel

45°

P.S. <u>Take heart</u>

African Bamboo Pipes come in all lengths and widths and unscaled notes without measurements or worry or limitations. We made pretty good sounds at Little Red School House in New York - Music is Music!
and who says we should limit sound to the western scale?

See Margaret Galloway's instructions: <u>Making and Playing Bamboo Pipes</u>. Dryad Press · Leicester, England · for more serious musicians!

TIN CAN LANTERNS

Tin cans. Tin snips
nails. Hammer. string.

1. Fill can with water
2. Put cans to freeze (approx. 2 days)
3. draw design on can
   with crayon or marker
4. Put frozen can on pillow or
   towel so it won't roll.
5. Use BIG and small nail
   holes for variation
6. Use thin coat hanger wire
   for handles & hanging loops

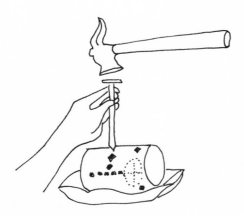

Do several at
once. To
control melting
refreeze and
take another
can to work on.

KEEP LIDS.
for ornaments
* see what the
beer can opener
will do.

TIN LID ORNAMENTS

OWL

CUT
on
RED
LINE

Angel

1. Put flat lid on pounding surface & Hammer nail holes with nail point and Long holes with nail head

2. Round body over hammer handle

THE CLIMBING PULL TOY

use a coping saw, drill, string.
wood 6" x 8" x 1". 2 Beads or
buttons. cup hook. felt marker
and a 7" x 1" wooden stick for
the holding bar.

1. Draw a figure on a piece of wood.
2. Cut out figure with a coping saw
3. Drill holes in hands of figure *
4. Drill 3 holes in holding bar
   at each end and in the cente
5. Cut 2 pieces of string, 5' long
6. Thread string through holdi
   bar and tie a knot on top.
   Thread strings through
   hand holes of figure
   and tie a bead or
   button at end of
   string.
7. screw cup hook
   overhead in
   center of
   doorway
8. Attach holding
   bar to hook.

Holding Bar →

← 6"

drill hand holes.

8"

6"

ACTION:

Pull strings
alternating
Left and right.
Watch your figure
Climb up the strings.
Relax tension to see
figure slide down.

THE FLAPPING OWL

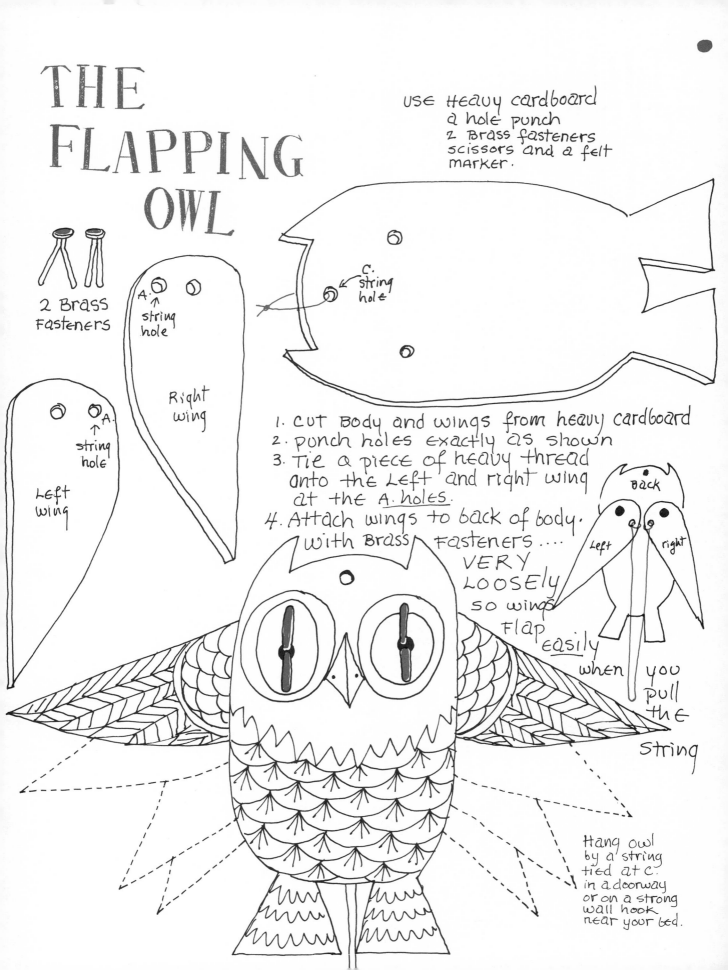

USE Heavy cardboard
a hole punch
2 Brass fasteners
scissors and a felt
marker.

2 Brass Fasteners

A.
string
hole

Right wing

A.
string
hole

Left wing

C.
string
hole

1. Cut Body and wings from heavy cardboard
2. Punch holes exactly as shown
3. Tie a piece of heavy thread onto the Left and right wing at the A. holes.
4. Attach wings to back of body. with Brass Fasteners .... VERY LOOSELY so wings Flap easily when you pull the string

back

Left   right

Hang owl by a string tied at c. in a doorway or on a strong wall hook near your bed.

HAMMERED WIRE JEWELRY

thin & heavy brass & copper wire.
thin-nosed pliers. Hammer. Anvil
or metal slab. earring backs.

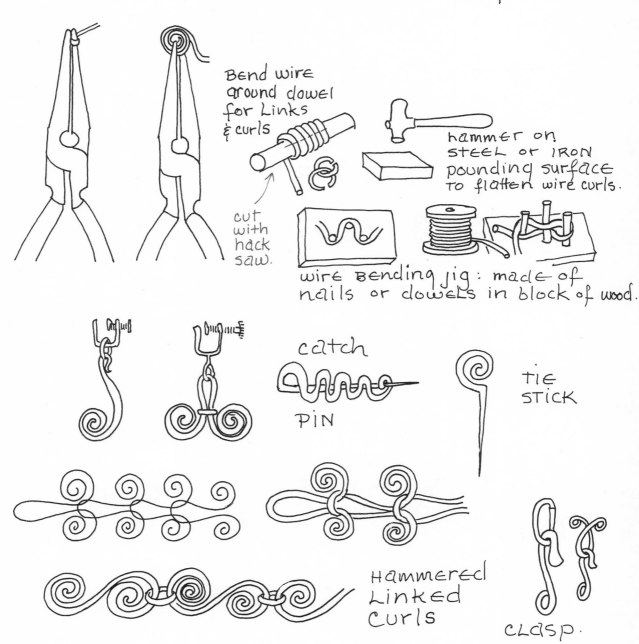

Bend wire around dowel for Links & curls

cut with hack saw.

hammer on STEEL or IRON pounding surface to flatten wire curls.

wire BENDING jig: made of nails or dowels in block of wood.

catch

PIN

tie STICK

Hammered Linked Curls

clasp.

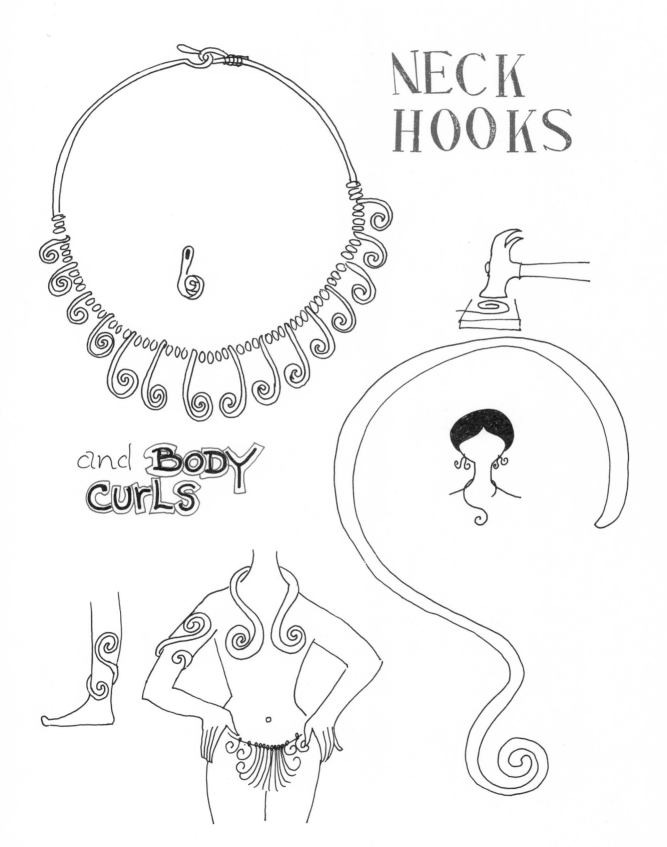

NECK HOOKS

and BODY CURLS

LOVE BEADS

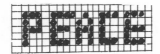

Use Indian beads and nylon monofilament for stringing. And a graph pattern

An exercise in counting stringing and secret messages.

Graph Pattern first

Row
1
2
3
4
5

5 or 7 line blocks are best for the letters of the alphabet.

1. choose two colors of beads one for message one for background.
2. measure thread or monofilament 5 times around your hand
3. string background beads, about 25 and start message
4. count message beads in your graph pattern, and string colors accordingly.
5. after each row string enough background color beads to cover back of hand around to the beginning of row 2
6. when all rows are strung tie string ends together and wrap beads around the neck of the one you love.

PASTA BEADS & PAPERCLIPS

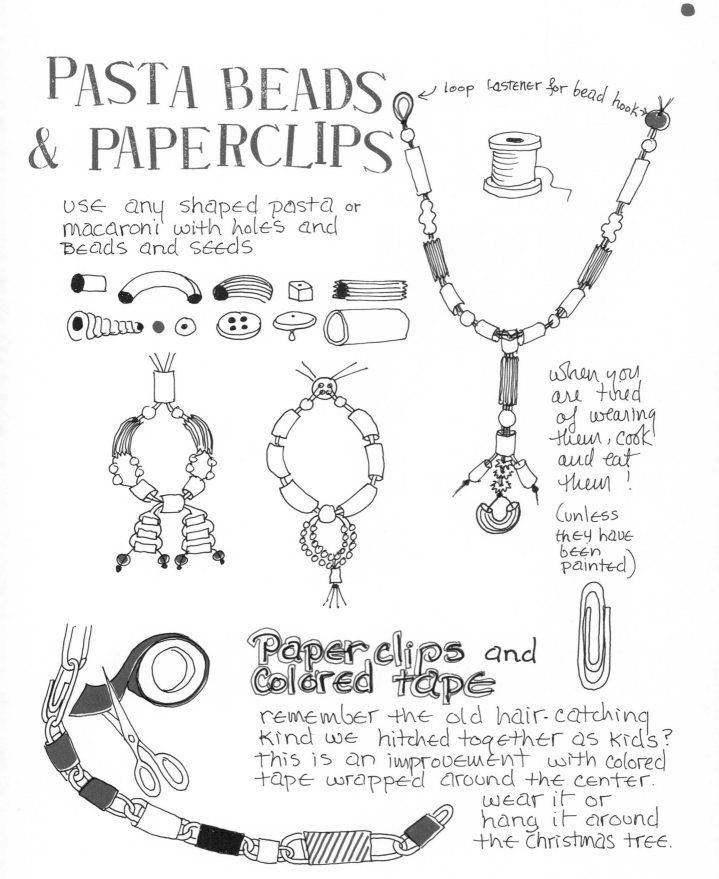

loop ← fastener for bead hook →

USE any shaped pasta or macaroni with holes and Beads and seeds

when you are tired of wearing them, cook and eat them!

(unless they have been painted)

Paperclips and Colored tape

remember the old hair-catching kind we hitched together as kids? this is an improvement with colored tape wrapped around the center.
wear it or hang it around the christmas tree.

BALANCE

- Little and heavy balance Big and light.

1. feather
2. paper clips · clay ball and a clay stand

Straighten clips stick one end into feather + the other end into clay ball

make a loop in the middle of wire so it can hang on the hook of the wire stand.

1 cork
2 dried prunes
2 paper clips
1 straight pin.

BALANCING TOYS

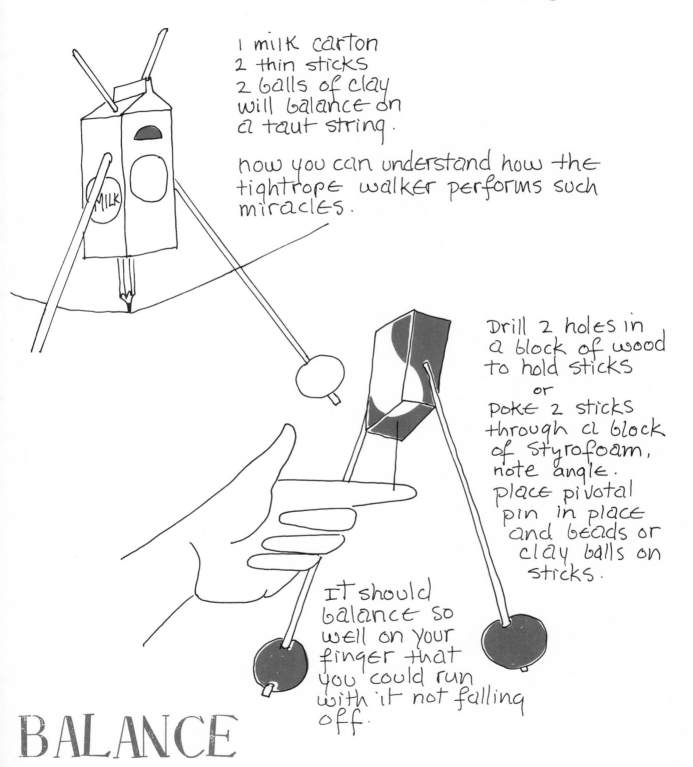

1 milk carton
2 thin sticks
2 balls of clay
will balance on
a taut string.

now you can understand how the
tightrope walker performs such
miracles.

Drill 2 holes in
a block of wood
to hold sticks
or
poke 2 sticks
through a block
of styrofoam,
note angle.
place pivotal
pin in place
and beads or
clay balls on
sticks.

It should
balance so
well on your
finger that
you could run
with it not falling
off.

BALANCE

SALT PENDULUM

Use an ordinary small funnel or cone of heavy paper taped closed with cut nose.
ordinary table salt.
string and black paper.
2 cup hooks.

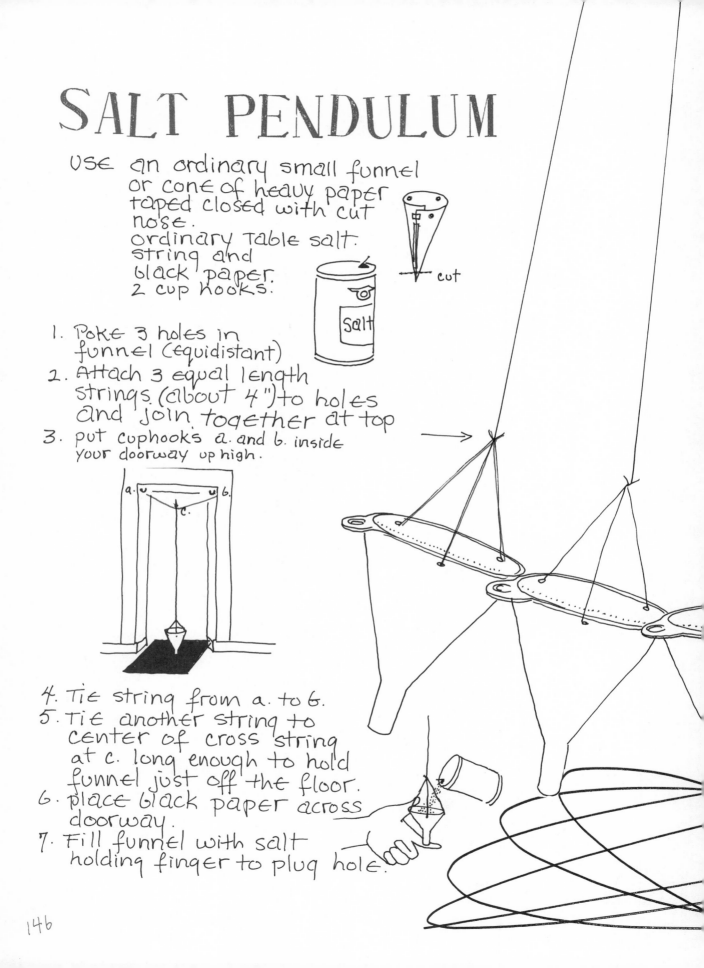

1. Poke 3 holes in funnel (equidistant)
2. Attach 3 equal length strings (about 4") to holes and join together at top
3. put cuphooks a. and b. inside your doorway up high.

4. Tie string from a. to b.
5. Tie another string to center of cross string at c. long enough to hold funnel just off the floor.
6. place black paper across doorway.
7. Fill funnel with salt holding finger to plug hole.

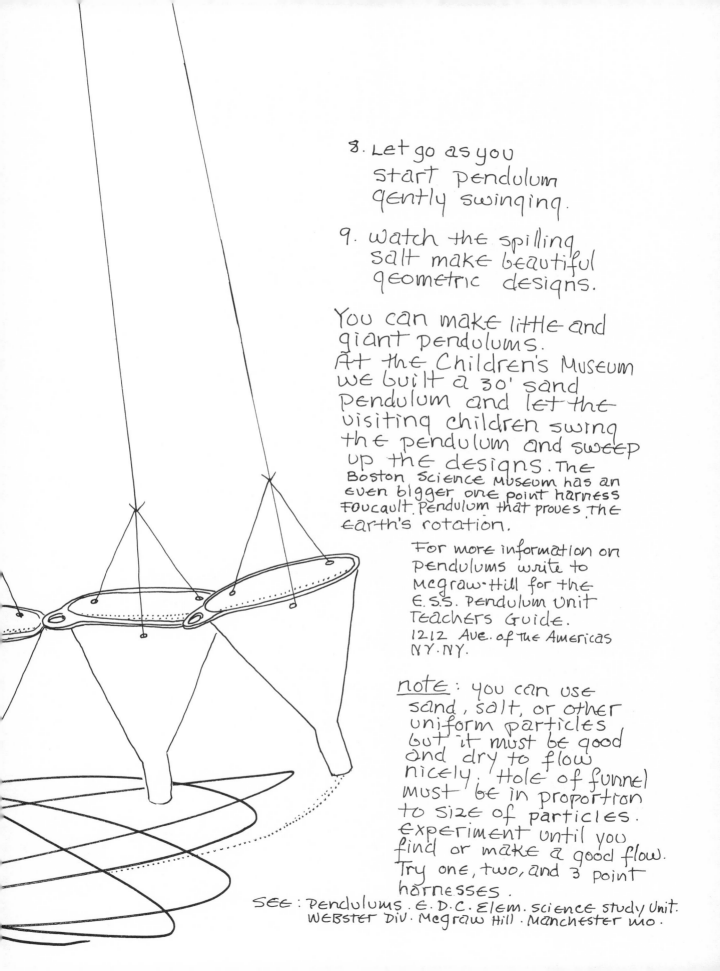

8. Let go as you start pendulum gently swinging.

9. Watch the spilling salt make beautiful geometric designs.

You can make little and giant pendulums.
At the Children's Museum we built a 30' sand pendulum and let the visiting children swing the pendulum and sweep up the designs. The Boston Science Museum has an even bigger one point harness Foucault Pendulum that proves the Earth's rotation.

For more information on pendulums write to McGraw-Hill for the E.S.S. Pendulum Unit Teachers Guide.
1212 Ave. of the Americas N.Y. N.Y.

note: you can use sand, salt, or other uniform particles but it must be good and dry to flow nicely. Hole of funnel must be in proportion to size of particles. Experiment until you find or make a good flow. Try one, two, and 3 point harnesses.

SEE: Pendulums. E.D.C. Elem. science study Unit. Webster Div. McGraw Hill. Manchester mo.

CANDLE DIPPING

USE: a box of paraffin wax
2 coffee cans
Hot plate or stove
candle wicking or string
crayon bits for color

1. Fill one coffee can full of cold water
2. Fill second can ¾ full of water and heat on stove in double boiler
3. Put paraffin slab into heating water. Allow wax to melt
4. Prepare wick: cut twice the depth of the can about 12" for a double candle. 6" for single candle.
5. Hold wick in the center, dip into hot wax and then into cold water. (Pull wick straight.) Go back and forth until your candle grows to the size you like.
6. Cut your 2 candles apart and have dinner by candle-light. And remember this was early man's first fire keeper and night light. The candle: wick in wax, enabled man to extend his workday and see in the dark!

wax {
water {
stove →
cold water

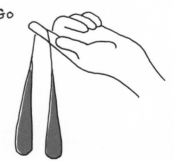

master notes and Caution : Paraffin is dangerous. never boil or over heat, only melt. wax can ignite and smoke terribly. Always use a double boiler. warm wax makes a better candle than hot wax. wax fires must be smothered - remove smoking wax out of doors.

caution · caution · caution · caution · caution · caution · caution · · · ·

CANDLE CASTING

in wet sand

1. Fill a box with sand.
2. Add enough water to dampen sand.
3. Scoop out a hole or screw your fist in the sand.
4. Poke thumb and 2 fingers into hole, down far enough to make leg molds.
5. Melt paraffin in double boiler. Melt crayon bits for color.
6. Pour melted wax into mold.
7. While wax is soft make wick hole with toothpick
8. Introduce wick into candle. pour tiny bit more warm wax to set wick.
9. When wax is cool remove candle from sand. Make different shapes.

make mold with fist and fingers.

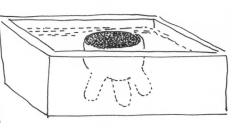

cut wick

master notes: The sand sticks to the outside of candle

If you want a wider sand area mix a can of sand and wax together and coat the hole with a thick wall of this mix. Then pour pure wax into center burning area.

wick can be introduced at pouring stage by tying section of wick to stick and resting it over the wax hole. Pour slowly so wick stands straight.

Add candle hardener for better, longer burning candles.
½ lb. stearic acid per 11 pound block of paraffin.

149

STAINED GLASS

COOKIES

EASY

crushed candy
PEACE and LOVE
COOKIES

1. USE a plain cookie mix
   or this basic RECIPE:
   ⅓ Cup vegetable shortening
   ⅓ cup sugar
   1 egg
   3 Cups Flour (sifted — all purpose)
   ½ tsp. baking soda sifted with flour
   1 tsp. salt scant
   ⅔ cup honey

2. Mix and roll dough into
   sausage strips about
   ¼" thick for strong
   outlines. Be sure pieces
   connect for strength.

3. Make designs on
   aluminum foil over
   cookie sheet.

   (it may help to chill dough before
   rolling.)

4. <u>Colored filling</u> : crack up lollipops, sprinkle in openings.
5. <u>Bake</u> : at 375° about 8 to 10 minutes.
6. <u>Cool</u> — then peel off aluminum foil when dough is firm.

note : don't make stained glass sculpture bigger than your oven!

7. <u>Sticks</u> : cookies can be baked with or without sticks.
Sticks can be baked in place if your oven is big enough. or press stick into cookie while it is still warm and soft.

Use ⅛" or ¼" wooden dowels.

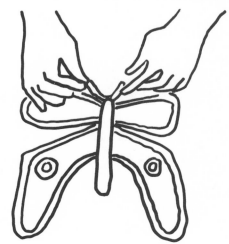

Ilse invented this cookie innovation — what a beautiful discovery!
Ilse and Philip Johnson, both artists, have wonderful <u>Bake-ins</u> and invite neighboors and friends to discover their own talents.

See: <u>Cookies & Breads</u> <u>The Baker's Art</u>. Reinhold.

Inedible
BAKER'S CLAY PLAYDOUGH

A. **Baker's clay**
   4 cups flour
   1 cup salt
   1½ cups water

Mix and knead, if too stiff add water.
Shape into figures
Bake 1 hour in 300° oven or until hard
when cold, paint and decorate.
To keep, spray with fixative or shellac.
Dough will keep moist in plastic bag.

B. **Cornstarch clay**
   2 parts table salt
   1 part cornstarch
   1 part water

Mix and cook over low heat
until stiff. Add a few drops of
cooking oil to delay drying.
Shape figures when cool
Let dry 2 days or 1 hour in oven.

C. **Sugar Dough** : (for very little children who might eat it.)
   1 cup water
   2 cups suger
   3 cups flour

mix as you do the salt dough (A.)
It is less durable but safer if
eaten.

Color can be added to all of these recipes
Vegetable coloring is best

Edible
BREAD DOUGH SCULPTURE

Bread: the staff of life and the bond of friendship.
To break it is to share. To make it is to care.

Basic bread recipe:
1 package yeast
2 cups warm water
3 Tablespoons sugar or honey
2 teaspoons salt
1/4 cup oil
7 cups flour

start yeast in warm sugar water
Let stand 5 minutes, (to start yeast working.)
Add salt oil and flour,
a little at a time until you can
work dough with your hands.
If sticky add more flour
Knead and make sculpture.
on cookie sheet or aluminum foil.

Dough sculpture must lie flat, not standing.
make pancake, snakes and ball shapes
stick them together with a little water or lick
your finger. Parts will grow together as the
dough rises. Let rise 10 to 20 min. Bake at 350°
20 to 30 min. depending on size of figure.

To celebrate the opening of the
"Art Food and Technology" Exhibit
at the Institute of Contemporary Art
in Boston, Drago's Bakery and I
made a 5' 25. pound Bread Mermaid.
she was eaten in 20 minutes
at midnight.

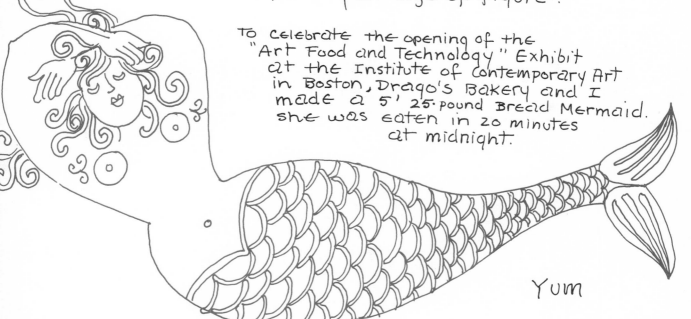

Yum

PEACEABLE BREAD

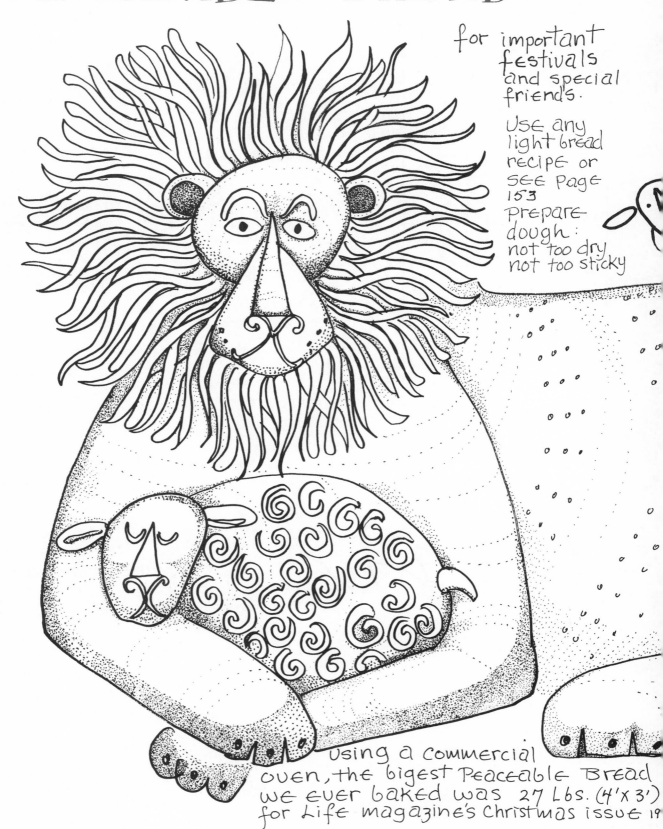

for important festivals and special friend's.

Use any light bread recipe or see page 153 prepare dough: not too dry not too sticky

Using a commercial oven, the bigest peaceable bread we ever baked was 27 Lbs. (4'x 3') for Life magazine's Christmas issue 19

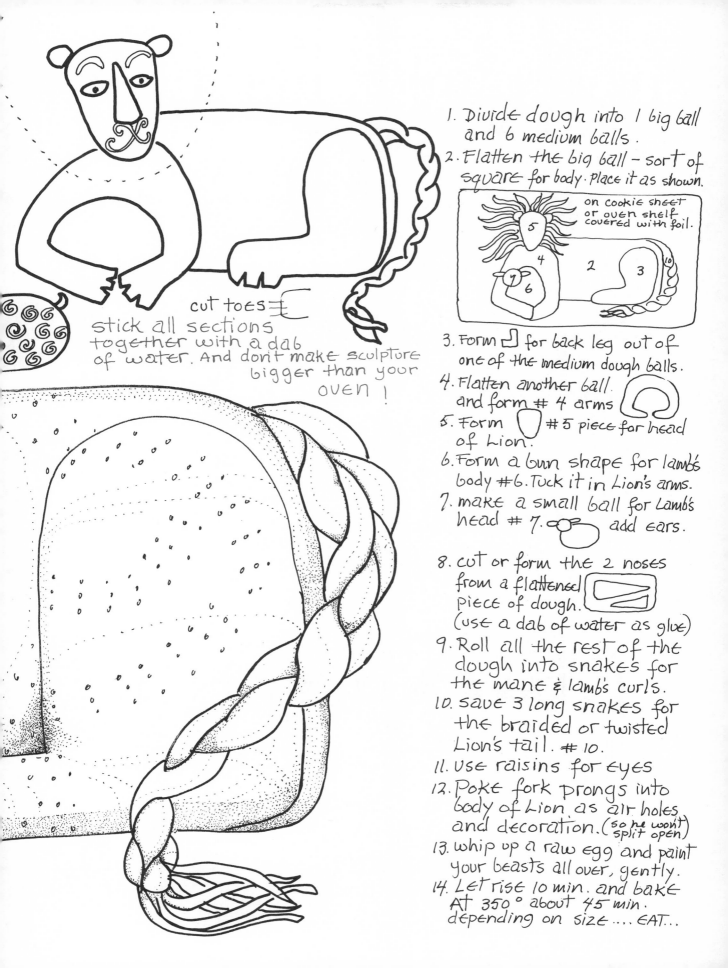

cut toes

stick all sections together with a dab of water. And don't make sculpture bigger than your oven !

1. Divide dough into 1 big ball and 6 medium balls.
2. Flatten the big ball — sort of square for body. Place it as shown.

on cookie sheet or oven shelf covered with foil.

3. Form ⌐ for back leg out of one of the medium dough balls.
4. Flatten another ball and form #4 arms
5. Form ▽ #5 piece for head of Lion.
6. Form a bun shape for lamb's body #6. Tuck it in Lion's arms.
7. make a small ball for Lamb's head #7. add ears.

8. cut or form the 2 noses from a flattened piece of dough. (use a dab of water as glue)
9. Roll all the rest of the dough into snakes for the mane & lamb's curls.
10. save 3 long snakes for the braided or twisted Lion's tail. #10.
11. use raisins for eyes
12. Poke fork prongs into body of Lion as air holes and decoration. (so he won't split open)
13. whip up a raw egg and paint your beasts all over, gently.
14. LET rise 10 min. and bake AT 350° about 45 min. depending on size.... EAT...

MORE
ART & CRAFT BOOKS

Atwater	Byways in Handweaving, Macmillan
Biegeleisen	Silk Screen Printing & production. Dover
Birrell	The Textile Arts. Harper & Row
Blumenau	Creative Design in Wallhangings. Crown
Brown & Ellenberger	Atlas of Animal Anatomy for Artists. Dover
Coats & Clark #170 B	LEARN How BOOK (Knit & crochet)
Davenport	Your Hand Spinning. Craft & Hobby book Serv.
de Dellmont	Encyclopedia of Needlework. D.M.C. corp
Di Valentin	Practical Encyclopedia of Crafts. Sterling
Forman & Wissa Wassef	Tapestries from Egypt by Children. Hamlyn
Gray	Gray's Anatomy, Lea & Febiger
Harvey	Macrame, Reinhold
Herberts	The complete Book of Artists Techs. Praeger
Hils	Creative Crafts, Reinhold
Hunt	25 Kites that fly. Dover
Johnson & Hazelton	Cookies & Breads etc. Reinhold
Kampmann	Creating with puppets. Van Nostrand -"
Kreischer	Symmography. Crown
Krevitsky	Stitchery: Art & Craft. Van Nost.-Reinhold
Krevitsky	Batik: Art & Craft. Van Nostrand Reinhold
LaLiberte &McIlhany	Banners & Hangings. Reinhold
Lanteri	Modelling & Sculpture Vol.1-3. Dover

Laury	oll Making; a creative approach . Van Nostrand-Rein
Lesch	Vegetable Dyeing . Watson & Guptill
Lovoos & Paramore	Modern Mosaic Techniques . Watson & Guptill
Maryon	Metalwork & Enameling . Dover
Meilach	Creating Art from Anything . Reilly & Lee
Meilach	Macrame : Creative design in Knotting . Crown
Nelson	Ceramics , A Potter's Handbook . Holt
Newman	Creative Candlemaking . Crown
Pluckrose	Introducing Crayon Technique . Watson & Guptill
Regensteiner	The Art of Weaving . Van Nostrand-Reinhold
Rieger	Raku Art & Technique . Reinhold
Rosenberg	Children make murals & Sculpture . Reinhold
Rosenbud & Wiener	Illustrated Hassle Free Make Your Own Clothes Book . Avenel
Sunset	Craft Series . Golden Press .
Stribling	Art from Found Materials . Crown
Supensky	Ceramic Art in the School Program
Untracht	Metal Techniques for Craftsmen . Doubleday
Wagner	Modern Carpentry . Goodheart Willcox
Willcox	Modern Leather design . Watson
Wilson	Weaving is for Anyone . Van Nostrand Reinhold
Wiseman	Rag Tapestries & Wool Mosaics . Van Nostrand-Rein.
Wright	The Complete Guide to Basket Weaving . Drake
Znamerowski	Step by Step Rug Making . Golden

BOOKS
ON WAYS OF LEARNING

Ashton-Warner   Teacher. Simon & Schuster
Axeline   Dibs, in search of self. Ballantine
Bowen   Froebel & self-education through Activity, Scribner's
Brearley & Hitchfield   Guide to Reading Piaget, Schocken
Charbonneau   Learning to Think in a Math Lab. NAIS
Cremins   The Transformation of the schools, Knopf
Dennison   The Lives of Children. Random House
Dewey   Schools of Tomorrow. Dutton
Erikson   Childhood & Society. Norton
ESS   The ESS Reader. Education Development Cent.
ESS   A Working guide to Elem. Science Study. McGraw-Hill
Featherstone   Schools where Children Learn. Liveright
Fraiberg   The Magic Years. Scribner's
Froebel   Education of Man. Appleton
Furth   Piaget for Teachers. Prentice-Hall
Ginsburg & Opper   Piaget's Theory of Intellectual Devlp. Prentice-Hall
Hartley & Goldenson   The Complete Book of Children's Play. Apollo Edit.
Hawkins   The Logic of Action, El. Sci. Adv. Ctr. U. of Colo.
Herndon   The Way It Spozed to Be. Simon & Schuster
Holt   How Children Fail. Dell
Isaacs   Intellectual growth in Young Children. Routledge
Isaacs   Social Development in Young Children. Schocken
Kohl   36 Children. New American Library.

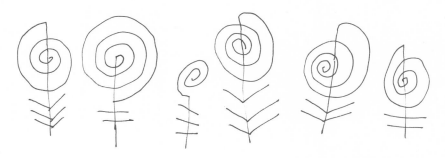

Kozol	Death at an Early Age . Houghton Mifflin
Leonard	Education & Ecstasy . Dell
Lowenfeld	Creative & Mental Growth . Macmillan
Maccoby & Zellner	Experiment in Primary Ed . Harcourt Brace Jovanovich
Marshall	An Experiment in Education . Camb. Univ. Press.
Moffatt	A Student Centered Language Arts Curric. Houghton Mifflin
Montessori	Spontaneous Activity in Education . Schocken
Murrow	Children Come First . American Heritage
Nuffield	I Do & I Understand . John Wiley
Nyquist, ed.	Open Education . Bantam
Postman & Weingarten	Teaching as a Subversive Activity . Delta
Pratt	I Learn from Children . Corner Stone Library
Read	Education Through Art . Pantheon
Richardson	In the Early World . Pantheon
Sargent	The Integrated Day in an Amer. School . NAIS
Schools Council Service	Informal Schools in Britain Today . Citation
Sharp	Thinking is Child's Play . Dutton
Smilansky	Play . Pamphlet . NAEYC
Sproul	With a Free Hand . Reinhold
Synectics, Inc.	Making it Strange . Harper & Row
Talbot	The World of the Child . Doubleday
Toffler	Future Shock . Random House
Way	Development Through Drama . Longman
Yeomans	Education for Initiative & Responsibility . NAIS

NEVER

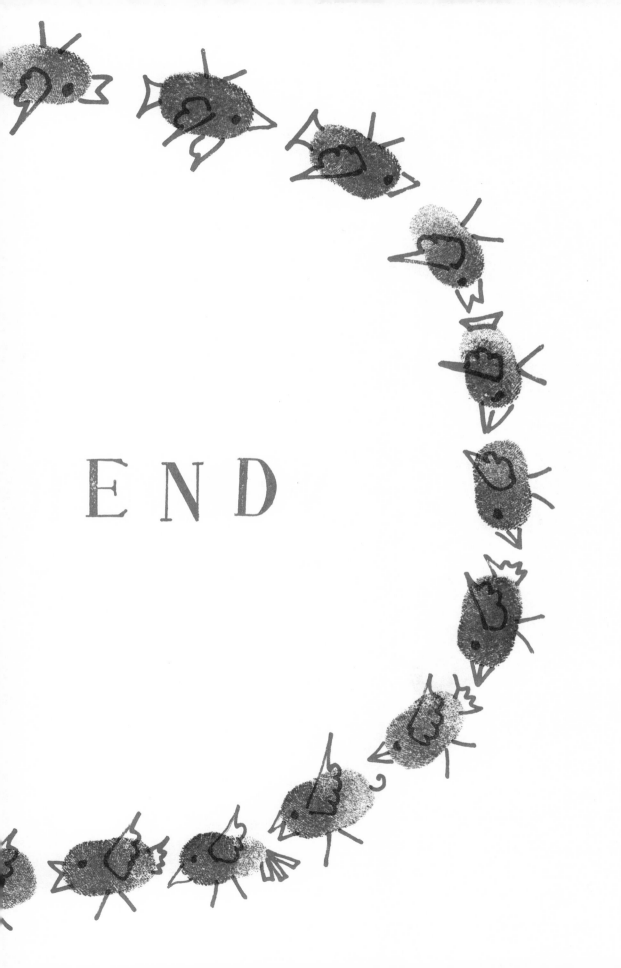

END

INDEX

Alaskan bow drill, 76
animals: birds, 59, 121; caterpillar, 121; fish, 27, 48-49; horses, 66-67, 121; owl, 139; rabbit, 121; slotted, 58-59 turtle's, 86-87
appliqué, 62-63
avocado pear tree, 126-127

bamboo: shepherd's pipe, 135
batik: cloth & hot wax resist, 114 crayon wax resist, 57, 114
belts: macramé, 101; twisted string, 88; inkle, 94
boxes: costumes, 120; horse, 67; house, 65; looms, 90, 94-95 sculpture, 121
bread: dough sculpture, 153; peaceable, 154-155

candles: casting, 149; dipping, 148
car, see go-car
cardboard: box costumes, 120; box sculpture, 121; corrugated cut-away, 36-37; flapping owl, 139; fold & cut, 24-25; looms, 90; portable houses, 64-65; printing, 37; racing turtles, 86-87; slotted animals, 58-59
casting: candles, 149; plaster, 128; sand, 129
clothing: belts, 95; body covering, 108 caftan & burnoose 109, 110; coat, 110; coolie pants & jacket, 109; dashiki, 109; dress, 110; foot gloves, 116-117, hats, 78; quick, 109-110; rebozo, 110; robe, 110, sandals, 79; shirt, 110 vest, 107

color: mixing, 53
cookies: stained glass, 150-151
costumes: cardboard, 120; clothes, 108-109
crayons: rubbings, 57; scratch board, 56; stained glass, 56; wax resist batik, 57

decorations: see ornaments
dolls: bed friends, 60; umm-dears, 60
doll houses: 64-65
dough: bread sculpture, 153-154; play, 153
drawing: crayons, 56-57; on window shades, 54-55; see also painting
drill: Alaskan bow, 76; coathanger, 77

fish: printing, 48-49; tissue, 27
flowers: to dry, see weed keeper
foot risers: 71; stilts, 70-71

gloves: finger puppets, 123
go-car, 69
grass mats, 78

hammer, see tools
heddle, 91; popsicle stick loom, 93
houses: box, 65; cardboard, 64; doll, 64-65; plywood, 64

jewelry: hammered wire, 140-141; macramé necklace, 162

kites: 84-85
knots: half hitch, 100; Oriental, 106; rya, 106; spiral, 101; square, 100

lantern - tin can, 136
leaf skeletons, 80

looms: belt, 92; board & nail, 90; frame, 90; hanging stick, 90; inkle, 94-95; Japan Nissan Island bow, 98; macramé keel, 104; Navaho crotch, 99; oatmeal box, 90; paper plate, 90; plank, 90; plastic straw, 92; popsicle stick, 93; Y branch, 90

macramé: 100-105; belt, 101; half hitch, 100; keel loom, 104; knee harness, 100; Love Pouch, 103; necklace, 102; sailor's lace, 100; square knot, 100

masks: paper, 31; stocking, 118-119
mats, see grass mats
movies, 82-83
musical instruments: found objects, 133; shepherd's pipe, 135; thumb piano kaffir, 134; xylophone, 132

necklaces: love beads, 142; macramé, 102; neck hooks, 141; pasta beads & paperclips, 143

orange crates: box horse, 67; skooter, 68
ornaments: clothespin butterfly, 73; paper, 18-19; tin lid, 137

painting: for beginners, 52-53; chocolate pudding, 50-51;
finger, 50; on window shades, 54-55

paper: bag puppets, 34-35; birds, 59; curls & mobiles 26; cutting, 20-21; faces, 30-31; fold & cut, 24-25; gliders, 28; kites, 84; lace hangers, 16-17; making, 14-15; masks 30-31; ornaments, 18-19 plate loom, 90; sculpture, 21; spinners, 29; tissue fish, 27; towel dyeing, 113; village, 22-23; weaving, 90; whistle, 73

paperclips: & bead necklace, 143; & tape necklace, 143
pendulum: salt, 146-147
pillow cozies, 61
pipe: xylophone, 132; shepherd's 135; bubble, 124
plaster: carving blocks, 131; casting, 128; printing 46-47; sand casting, 129, scrimshaw, 130
plastic bag: kite, 85
plants, see avocado pear tree
playdough: baker's clay, 152; cornstarch clay, 152; sugar dough 152
popsicle sticks: loom, 93; thumb piano kaffir, 134
printing: block, 46-47; chocolate pudding, 50-51; finger, 38-39; fish, 48-49, foot, 40-41; hand, 40; potato, 45; roller, 44 vegetables, 40-43

puppets : finger, 32-33 ; glove, 123 ;
    paper bag, 34-35 ; sock, 122

rope winding, 89
rubbings : 57

sand : casting, 129 ; pendulum, 146-147
saw, 75
scratch boards, 56 ; printing, 46-47
scrimshaw : plaster, 130
sculpture : box, 121 ; bread dough, 153-
    155 ; egg carton, 121 ; paper,
    21 ; playdough, 152
sgraffito, 56
shepherd's pipe, 135
skooter : skate & orange crate, 68
slotted animals : 58
soap bubbles, 124
socks : puppets, 122
stilts, 70-71
stitchery, 62
string twisting, 88

tie-dye ; 112-113
tin : fold & cut, 24-25
tin can : foot risers, 71 ; lanterns 136
tools : Alaskan bow drill, 76 ; coat
    hanger bow drill, 77 ; hammer,
    74 ; saw, 75
toys : balancing, 145 ; button spinner,
    73, clothespin butterfly, 73 ;
    climbing pull, 138 ; cork copter,
    73 ; flapping owl, 139, spinning
    top, 73 ; walking spool, 73

vegetables : printing, 40-43, 45

weaving : 90-99 ; in math 96-97
    weed, 98-99
weed keeper, 81, see also leaf
    skeletons
weeds : hats, 78 ; keeper, 81 ; mats,
    78 ; soles, 79 ; weaving 98-99
whistles : paper, 73 ; willow, 72
wire : bubble pipes, 124 ; coat
    hanger drill, 77 ; jewelry,
    140-141 ; stocking masks, 118
wood : bo'sun's macramé keel
    loom, 104-105 ; box horse,
    67 ; climbing pull toy, 138 ;
    horse bench, 66, portable
    house, 64 ; printing, 46-47 ;
    stilts, 70-71

xylophone : 132